YORK NOTE

General Editors: Professor
of Stirling) & Professor Suh
University of Beirut)

Douglas Dunn

SELECTED POEMS

Notes by Alasdair Macrae

Senior Lecturer in English Studies, University of Stirling

LONGMAN
YORK PRESS

YORK PRESS
Immeuble Esseily, Place Riad Solh, Beirut

LONGMAN GROUP UK LIMITED
Longman House, Burnt Mill,
Harlow, Essex CM20 2JE, England
Associated companies, branches and representatives
throughout the world

First published 1993

ISBN 0–582–21537–4

Phototypeset by Gem Graphics, Trenance, Mawgan Porth, Cornwall
Printed in Singapore

Contents

Part 1

Introduction

The life and background of Douglas Dunn

When *Elegies* was published in 1985, critics compared the collection to Tennyson's *In Memoriam*, the most significant poem of the Victorian period, and to Hardy's extraordinary 'Poems of 1912–13', written in troubled memory of his first wife. These comparisons, linked with the popular success of *Elegies* and the acclaim of winning the Whitbread Award, have set Dunn very high in contemporary poetry.

Douglas Eaglesham Dunn was born in 1942 in a small village in Renfrewshire called Inchinnan, a few miles west of the centre of Glasgow. His father worked in a tyre factory, eventually in a supervisory capacity. It was his belief in education that Dunn looks back on as a major shaping influence, and it was he who taught the young boy to read at the age of four. After attending the local schools, Dunn trained as a librarian and it was as a librarian that he spent a year in the United States. On his return to Britain he moved to Hull to take a university degree in English. The University Librarian in Hull was Philip Larkin, a poet much admired by him, who was later to become a close friend when Dunn obtained a job in the university library; they also shared a love of jazz.

In 1969 Dunn's first book of poems, *Terry Street*, was published by Faber and Faber, the most prestigious publishers of poetry in Britain. It received some lavish praise in reviews by influential critics, and his career as a writer was successfully launched. In 1971 he gave up his job as a librarian to concentrate on writing. By this time he was married. His second volume, *The Happier Life*, appeared in 1972 and was followed by *Love or Nothing* (1974). A longer interval elapsed before *Barbarians* (1979), followed in 1981 by *St Kilda's Parliament*. Also in 1981 his wife Lesley, the Senior Keeper at Hull Art Gallery, died of cancer, and he returned to live in Scotland. He made a living by working as a writer in residence, giving readings, and by literary journalism, particularly book reviewing. Earlier he had edited a selection of Byron's verse and a book of essays called *Two Decades of Irish Writing*, and had written a considerable number of short stories, mainly for the *New Yorker*. A long sequence poem, *Europa's Lover*, was published in 1982, and in 1984 BBC Television showed *Anon's People*, a programme of archive films going back over sixty years, with accompanying poems written by Dunn.

1985 saw the publication of two major works: *Secret Villages*, a collection of sixteen of his short stories, and *Elegies*, poems written in memory of his wife. In the following year his standing was recognised with the publication of the very substantial *Selected Poems 1964–1983*. Since then he has been prolific in his writing and as an editor. A book of poems, *Northlight*, appeared in 1988, and a new collection, *Dante's Drum-Kit*, will be published in 1993. A translation of Racine's *Andromache* came out in 1990 and was produced on radio. Also in 1990 his pamphlet, *Poll Tax: The Fiscal Fake*, was issued as an argued attack on the Conservative government's community charge. Two strands of his thinking on the Scottish tradition have emerged in two anthologies: *Scotland: An Anthology* (1991), a collection of pieces, some by Scots, some by others, designed to show the essence of Scotland; and *The Faber Book of Twentieth-Century Scottish Poetry* (1992). Also in 1992, *Dressed to Kill*, a programme devised by him, was broadcast on television; it explores in pictures and verse something of the history and imagery of soldiery in Scotland. Over the years he has written half a dozen plays, mainly for radio and television.

Some years after the death of his first wife he remarried, and now has two children by his second wife, also named Lesley. In 1991 he became a professor at the University of St Andrews. He now lives in Tayport on the coast of Fife. His work has won many prizes, he has travelled widely, and his poetry has been translated into many languages. He is generally regarded as one of the leading poets writing in English, and his critical essays and reviews on other poets are treated with respect.

It is no mere coincidence that Dunn has spent the three main phases of his life on or near the estuaries of rivers: the Clyde in his youth; the Humber when he was a developing poet in Hull; and the Tay since his return to Scotland in 1981. He enjoys the idea of a river taking its origins in a hinterland and emerging into the ocean. That threshold between river and sea, between land and water, is like an image of tradition feeding into the present and anticipating the future. In many ways Dunn is a traditionalist, strongly conscious of a Scottish heritage and a poetic lineage. However, this does not mean that he is backward-looking in a nostalgic way; rather he is progressive and eager to develop a tradition. Furthermore, Inchinnan, where he was brought up, was neither city nor suburb nor town nor yet open, remote countryside but, at the time, had a sense of its own particularity. This feeling of distinctiveness is reflected in many poems in which Dunn shows a strong awareness of boundaries and territories, whether of class, language or ethos, which probably derives from the discriminations of which he became aware in his childhood. The people with whom he grew up would have spoken Scots, a regional dialect of English with distinctive vocabulary, grammatical forms and accent, and a considerable body of literature dating back to the fourteenth century.

those with inherited wealth and social position and argues for a socialist egalitarianism and a distribution of the wealth created by the work of the nation. His (Scottish) nationalism is similarly based on his sense of a complacent imbalance of power between England and Scotland, where the lesser partner is consistently ignored or patronised. The thrust of his politics is not to perpetuate a class struggle or a nationalist resentment but to expose and break the parochial attitudes of self-styled superior people and the mandarins in London for whom someone of a different class or outside London is bound to be inferior and insignificant.

His choice of Lord Byron (1788–1824) as a poet whose selected verse he edited is very appropriate to his socio-political attitude. Not that his poetry, any more than his character, resembles that of Byron, but Byron offers an example of a poet who exposed pomposity, hyprocrisy and petty-mindedness. In fact, Dunn does not often show the direct influence of earlier poets. In his liking for conducting a line of argument through a complicated verse-form he exhibits a link with seventeenth-century poets, and some of his pastoral poems, particularly in *Barbarians*, manifest a kinship with Andrew Marvell (1621–78) who also spent a substantial part of his life in Hull. The discursive, point-by-point quality of many of Dunn's poems has more in common with eighteenth-century rational poets such as Pope and Swift than with the system-builders and visionaries of the nineteenth-century Romantic period such as Blake, Wordsworth and Shelley. Of the later nineteenth-century poets, Browning, with his obliquenesses, his constructed personae, his sense of the speaking voice, would be more congenial than the more poetical and humourless Tennyson.

Twentieth-century poets usually regarded as major figures – Yeats, Pound, Eliot, Williams, Stevens, MacDiarmid – have had no obvious impact on Dunn's poetry, although they have contributed to the poetic climate in which he matured as a poet. Indeed, by the 1950s a reaction against Modernism had set in, and groups of poets in England – 'The Group' and 'The Movement' – seemed to turn against internationalism, romantic gesture, experiment, and large ambitions in poetry, and insist on localism, irony and laconic unexuberance. The poetry of Thomas Hardy (1840–1928) was elevated as a model and W. H. Auden (1907–73) was much admired. By the mid-1960s a new fashion emerged to challenge the timidity and calculated drabness of the previous decade, and the influence of William Carlos Williams (1883–1963), with his contemporary followers, the Beat poets such as Ginsberg and Ferlinghetti, came to be prominent. Douglas Dunn's earlier volumes tend to follow the Hardy–Auden line and eschew the ranting, incantatory style of the Beat poets and their British counterparts, for example, the so-called Liverpool Poets. His year in the United States had led him to read contemporary American poets such as Robert Lowell, John Berryman and, particularly, James

Wright who had grown up during the Depression of the 1930s in a small town in Ohio. In 1962 the critic A. Alvarez brought out an anthology entitled *The New Poetry*, in the introduction to which he condemned what he called the 'gentility principle' in contemporary English poetry and advocated an openness in poets to wider experiences and a loosening of forms. Dunn's early poetry, say to 1974, could not be labelled with the word 'gentility' but, equally, it was not in tune with much of the new fashion as represented in the anthology *The Children of Albion* (1969), edited by Michael Horovitz. Although similarities of phrase-making and tone certainly exist between Dunn's early poems and the poetry of Philip Larkin, and he has always declared his respect for the older poet, the poetic territory he chose for *Terry Street* was his own, and from that starting place he has developed very much in his own way. He is knowledgeable about the work of contemporary poets in many parts of the world but he does not belong to any very obvious group. Among the poets he admires are Seamus Heaney, Les Murray, Tony Harrison, Derek Mahon, Michael Longley.

Since returning to Scotland in 1981 he has involved himself more thoroughly in public affairs, mainly but by no means exclusively of a literary sort. Living in a small town he is a member of a community, and political issues have a very specific focus. Furthermore, Scotland is a tiny country in respect of population, and a literary figure can become known to a large proportion of its people beyond a circle of particular friends and neighbours. As a literary journalist in newspapers, television and radio, as a professor at Scotland's oldest university, as an active member of the Arts Council and as a performer of his poetry, Dunn has emerged as a recognisable personality. His socialist stance took a very public form in 1990 with his refusal to pay the new community charge or poll tax introduced by the Conservative government and with the publication of his fierce denunciation of the tax in a pamphlet. As an epigraph he quotes John Milton: 'Men who set their minds on main matters, and sufficiently urge them, in these most difficult times, I find not many.' This inclination to straight talking is also apparent in the introduction to, and the process of selection in, his *The Faber Book of Twentieth-Century Scottish Poetry*. He chose not to include poets merely because they had been prominent figures in literary circles: if he did not esteem their poems he excluded them. He was prepared to put his own poetic judgement on public trial and was not surprised or dismayed at being condemned by certain reviewers. If he does not give his praise readily, neither does he offer or look for flattery.

A note on the text

Dunn's publications are listed in Part 5. All of the poems discussed in Part 2, up to and including the poems from *Elegies*, are included in

Selected Poems 1964–1983. The remaining poems come from *Northlight*. There are no substantial differences between the original published versions of poems and the versions given in *Selected Poems*. It is appropriate for me to acknowledge the generous help of the poet while I was writing these Notes.

Part 2

Summaries
of SELECTED POEMS

Poems from *Terry Street* (1969)

About two-thirds of the poems in this collection are included in *Selected Poems 1964–1983*. One poem, 'Envoi', written in 1981, was added to *Selected Poems* as a postscript and acts as a comment on the poet's Terry Street phase. The original collection is divided into two sections: 'Part One: Terry Street poems' and 'Part Two'.

Terry Street was in a run-down, slum area of the city of Hull, but Dunn uses elements of it more to exemplify certain kinds of social behaviour typical in British cities in the 1960s than to offer a specific or intimate portrait of an actual street. He is not often obviously present in the poems in his own person: the comings and goings of the Street are observed by a narrator, usually through a window. This narrator is male, detached and a temporary resident, sometimes a subject of curiosity or amusement to the natives. He listens to different music and has different reading habits, but his job, if he has one, is not indicated. People are not identified by name but some relationships and connections are known. The Street has few links with the larger world; there are no references to abroad, myth, history, spiritual aspirations, high culture, national events. Dullness, squalor, cheap glamour, seedy sexuality are emphasised. The poems often work by presenting an assemblage of objects, actions, surfaces which stand for social tastes and habits.

Part Two, somewhat longer, contains several poems which, because of the nature of their content and their style, could fit easily into the Terry Street sequence. However, many of the poems in the second sequence have a wider range of references: in time, setting (both urban and rural) and language. Instead of being an objective commentator as he was previously, Dunn is much more at the centre of these poems. This is reflected in particular in the poems which relate to his family background and early life in Scotland.

Most of the poems are written in stanzas of regular length, varying from two-line to eight-line units. Rhyme is not employed and, although Dunn tends to favour lines in a poem of roughly similar length in terms of stresses, there is no sense of a mechanical obedience to a fixed form. The poems progress in a tidy, unostentatious way, line by line, item by item, carefully placed.

'The Patricians'

The old men of the town are described in their routines and attitudes. Their visit to the launderette is used to show a public side to what are very private lives. They stand apart from the younger life of the town.

COMMENTARY:

The irony of the title (see Notes below) is central to the functioning of the poem. In many societies it has been common for the older men to become the elders of the group, respected as advisers, law-makers and arbiters in disputes. In the area of Terry Street the old men struggle to retain a dignity (lines 9 and 19–20), but in this modern urban setting they are not granted a prestigious position by the younger people. There is no interaction with others and no mention of the jobs they had worked at or of their wives although, at the end of the poem, reference is made to their children, now middle-aged and living in a different part of the city. Like their underwear, they seem out of date and something of an embarrassment even to themselves. There is no future for the men who note the deaths of their contemporaries and take a meagre pride in outlasting the others. All energy and momentum have gone: they move in a 'low gear slowly' and everything in their lives is 'sagging' and 'muffled'. Even the mechanical beat of their watches is stronger than the beat of their hearts.

Dunn's poem progresses in three-line stanzas, the sentences forming a series of blunt statements which, in their clipped, unexpansive quality, convey a weariness as if they were reluctant to take a point any further. However, the poem is not unsympathetic or cynical. Only once, in stanza 6, does the poet involve himself directly when he feels chilled by the futility of the old men. In the following stanza, he even expresses a certain regard for them, 'the individualists of our time', and describes them as being beyond petty fashions and competitive aspirations. In the seven jabbing sentences of the final nine lines we are presented with different slants on the remaindered old men.

NOTES AND GLOSSARY:

Patricians: (from Latin *pater*: a father) in ancient Rome, members of one of the original families in the city; the word came to mean an aristocrat, or a person with inherited social power

Bendix: brand name of a washing-machine, and an early name for a launderette, a commercial establishment where clothes could be washed and dried in coin-operated machines

unmentionables: underwear (employed humorously), particularly

	men's long woollen undergarments, otherwise known as 'combinations' or 'long johns'
aromatic:	having a fragrant smell (of tobacco)
new estates:	on the outskirts of many British towns and cities after the Second World War areas of housing were built with public money to allow slum areas to be cleared. Younger families tended to be moved first, and this often led to estrangement between the older and younger generations

---

'A Removal from Terry Street'

This is a description of a family's move out of Terry Street. No reason is provided for the move, nor is any destination indicated.

COMMENTARY:
Like nomadic tribespeople or refugees, the family carry with them the basic materials of their life. In the first seven lines the emphasis is on the ordinariness of the scene, 'the usual stuff'. Culture or education is represented by 'Four paperback westerns', fictional stories of violence and daring in situations totally dissimilar to the context of Terry Street. Army surplus garments were worn in the 1950s partly as a fashion but more commonly out of financial necessity. Dunn presents the shabby situation in a series of economical images. The narrator obviously knows the family, knows the relationship of the 'whistling youths' to the wife who is their sister, knows the nuisance the couple's son has caused in the street and comments snidely on his departure (line 7). The emotional impact of the poem comes in the detail of the father pushing a lawnmower, and the incongruity of a lawnmower in a street with no grass. Terry Street has nothing to do with nature although, at night, a subterranean form of nature, the worm, asserts itself briefly. The image of someone pushing a lawnmower in this dead, denatured place suggests a glimmer of hope or aspiration to Dunn and he concludes the poem with a blessing, a hope for escape, 'I wish him grass'.

NOTES AND GLOSSARY:
| **westerns:** | novels, often of a crude sort, dealing with the white settlements and particularly clashes between cowboys and Indians in the western states of North America. Such novels were very popular with working-class male readers |
| **surplus ... jackets:** | since the Second World War huge amounts of equipment surplus to the needs of the American Army have been available at cheap prices in shops in |

Britain. The battle-jackets are usually of dull green heavy cotton

'Sunday Morning Among the Houses of Terry Street'

Sunday is presented much more as the end of the week than as the beginning of a new week. Terry Street is described in its off-duty aspects, the morning after the pursuits of Saturday night.

COMMENTARY:
There is no active verb in either of the first two stanzas, each a minimal sentence. Equally, there is no person and there is no sound or movement. The flow of week-day life seems to have ceased, and there is a sense of stagnancy in the street on Sunday morning. The debris of Saturday's activities is listed: 'Things doing nothing, ending, rejected'. From the third stanza we are introduced to the inhabitants of Terry Street, but their activities seem lacklustre and mechanical. In stanza 3 the revellers have lost their cheerfulness; their mirth at Saturday night's party is deflated in the cold light of the morning. Their attempts to look smart have now come apart: the men's ties have been discarded and the women's elaborate hair settings have fallen down. The word 'deceased' suggests that the hairdos had a temporary existence. The 'fogs' of line 9 are the blurred consciousness brought about by too much alcohol or too little sleep. In fact, the whole situation has the dulled quality of an alcoholic hangover, between sleep and wakedness, between one week and the next, or, like the radio (line 14), between one station and another. Some people are up but still wearing their pyjamas, some are up but have not put in their false teeth, some are still asleep in an attempt to recover from over-drinking but they are neither comfortably asleep nor properly awake. Dunn catches this transitional atmosphere in an accumulation of tired, sordid, unenergetic images. In the final ten lines the poem changes direction. However muted the Salvation Army is in the established sombre situation, at least they make a noise and they have a purpose in their activity. In the final two stanzas Dunn shifts the perspective. He sees all the rubbish, the spent quality of life, sinking into a great sewer or to the bottom of the ocean. Line 29 appears to rescue the city from this depressing image but, judging from what we have already seen in the poem of the lives of the people in Terry Street, we can conclude the poem only with the unsoftened, terrifying image of the final line, 'Beneath the street, a thundering of mud'.

NOTES AND GLOSSARY:
'Sunday Morning Among the Houses of Terry Street': there is something quaint or poetical about the title. Why does Dunn not call the poem 'Sunday Morning in Terry

Street'? It is designed to draw attention specifically to the houses, the homes of people, and 'Among the' suggests a visitor going from one to the other. Sunday, the Christian day of rest and also the day celebrated as the day of Christ's resurrection from death, is in the poem neither a day of satisfaction after a productive week's work nor a day of optimistic new beginnings

fag-packets: empty cigarette packets

Balls ... newspaper: fish and chips were always wrapped in sheets of newspaper when they were being carried from the shop. Before discarding the emptied package the eater has crushed it into a ball

bottles: empty milk bottles to be collected by the milkman

lav: working-class form of 'lavatory'

teeth: false teeth

blank sobriety: there are two possible meanings here: (1) their sleep could appear the opposite of their earlier obvious drunkenness; or (2) they wake up no longer drunk but in a stupefied, vacant state

mossy: furred or coated with the remnants and after-effects of their eating and drinking

Salvation Army: a Christian charitable organisation established in 1865 on semi-military lines, with officers and uniforms. It took Christian teaching to the poorest and most miserable areas of cities and preached and performed Salvationist music in the streets (hence 'brass' for brass band)

tubas: brass musical instruments

obbligatos: necessary part or accompaniment (musical term); the dogs are prompted to howl by the noise of the band

flush: the cleansing action of water in a lavatory

a sink: an area lower than the surrounding location to which all liquids sink; a cesspool into which foul matter runs

'Young Women in Rollers'

Aspects of Terry Street are observed by the narrator from his window. The young women have come in from elsewhere but they fit easily into the Street and conform to its expectations of how people behave. Their arrival is charted, a contrast between the women and the narrator is pointed to, and he imagines how he and they could come closer. The poem concludes with the contrast being redrawn, re-emphasised.

COMMENTARY:

The poem is written in four-line stanzas. No rhyme is employed and, although there is not a fixed metrical scheme, most of the lines have four or five main stresses. In two instances the punctuation and sense cross over the gap between stanzas; there is no mechanical obedience of punctuation unit to line unit, and in the second half of the poem there are more marked pauses, indicated by several full stops in some stanzas. This physical pattern is consonant with a pattern of thought and feeling. There is a steady, largely predictable sequence of observations in the first four stanzas. In stanza 6, the observer (and narrator) is himself observed, and this alteration of focus is reflected in a more speculative, querying tone and quicker shifts of thought in shorter syntactic units.

In the opening lines the scene is set: a mixture of elements inside the houses and in the street. The narrator, although detached from the environment, knows who various people are – 'their married friend', 'A landlord' – and he certainly recognises types. The women are presented as half vulgar, half unthinking, even innocent. They try to be fashionable but can afford to buy only the previous year's fashions or, perhaps, they can buy clothes only every second year. Stockings have to be reserved for evening wear only. It is as if they were off duty in the afternoon and, according to the narrator, they have about about them an air of abandon, at least when they are together.

The scene is, we are led to believe, typical but on this occasion the narrator is spotted behind his window by the passing women. His bookishness and liking for classical music separate him from the habits of the Street, and there is a contrast, in his mind, between the 'strong' and uninhibited women and the softness he senses that they find in him. He feels laughed at, mocked, exposed, and yet the women make a lasting impression, suggested in the phrases 'Stay patterned', 'something that floats' and 'monuments to entertainment'. Something in the otherness of their lives stirs a wish in him to go beyond his own confines and 'learn something new'. In the evening, after the preparations of the afternoon, the women, now rather mythologised in his mind, will defy the constraints of conventions and regulations. He too will be in a different, imaginative realm of his own.

NOTES AND GLOSSARY:

Rollers: plastic or metal cylindrical shapes used to make hair curly. (Wearing rollers or curlers in a public place was deemed to be a mark of working-class women and very vulgar according to middle- and upper-class people)

pacified: kept quiet (often used of rebellious or potentially violent people)

blackheads:	small greasy pimples on the skin, which appear black-tipped on the surface
minuet:	engage in a slow, stately dance for two people, particular to the eighteenth century
Mozart:	Wolfgang Amadeus Mozart (1756–91), Austrian composer of classical music including minuets
Third:	the Third Programme on BBC Radio, now called Radio Three, which specialises in broadcasting classical music
slum rent-masters:	people who make large profits by charging excessive rents for inferior properties
Pop:	popular music in contrast to classical music, which appeals to a smaller audience
hits:	favourite tunes in popular music

'Close of Play'

Set in the genteel suburb of an English city the poem presents images of a leisured, sporty, affluent style of living. However, there is also the indication of a hidden, subversive challenge to the complacent belief that nature is safely under control.

COMMENTARY:
The title offers an ambiguity. 'Close of Play' means the end of a day's play in a cricket match which will be resumed the following day, but the phrase could also mean the termination of playing (with the possible commencement of something more serious). Both senses of the phrase operate in the poem. In the first half of the poem there is a mingling of ordinary, apparently innocent or even idyllic images and suggestions of disquiet or fragility. These suggestions become much more explicit in the second half. However, even the opening image is ambivalent. Cricket is a quiet game played by cricketers wearing white on a carefully prepared pitch ('tended ground'), but tended ground can also describe a cemetery, and the cricketers are likened to ghosts in their manners, that is, in their way of dressing and behaving ('Wandering in white'). Is there a hint in this that cricket is a ritual surviving from an earlier way of living? And is this why it seems so special ('worth a week of evenings')? In line 7 the description of the sound of a tennis match operates in a two-edged way: 'vicious pluck' is a vivid evocation of the noise of a ball hit hard with a stringed racket; however, there is also a sense of violence and tearing. Similarly, in the following two lines, the runner is not just trotting along but 'contesting' and 'Fighting'. An ironic comparison with the mythological Bacchus exposes the affluent affectations of the young adults, and any suggestion of the wildness associated with the god is dismissed in the suburban sedate-

ness of lines 16–22. As darkness thickens, however, something which seemed repressed or rendered safe by human ordering emerges to reassert another force. The first hint of its emergence is in the discarded alcohol which 'become[s] alive, golden smells'. In the final six stanzas, the emphasis is on 'wildness', 'defiantly', 'less polite', 'menace', 'without manners', and all the aspects of domesticated nature conspire to overthrow the order imposed on them through cultivation by human beings. Some human beings, too, change sides and seek to break the decent, established rules in rape.

Behind the myth of Bacchus and his Greek equivalent, Dionysus, lies a struggle in life, both biological and psychological, between order and disorder, control and anarchy. The play *The Bacchae*, by the Greek dramatist Euripides (480–406BC) explores the theme of repression in an extraordinary way more than two thousand years before Sigmund Freud (1856–1939) made the subject central to his theory of psychology. In Dunn's poem, in the darkness of the night, the time of dreams, strange ideas can surface in the mind, odd disorders can be imagined.

NOTES AND GLOSSARY:

week of evenings:	a variation on the phrase 'month (or week) of Sundays', meaning a long wait
goosepimples:	(also 'goose flesh' or 'goose bumps') a bumpy condition of skin caused by sudden chill or fear
harrier:	a cross-country runner
toughminded fops:	a paradoxical phrase: toughminded means determined, obstinate; fops are men who have a tendency to be over-conscious of fashions in clothes and empty-headed
mini-Bacchus:	in Roman mythology Bacchus was the god of wine and fertility. He was worshipped by women, often depicted with long dishevelled hair, who danced themselves into a frenzy. 'Mini' is small-scale or reduced
scale:	a musical exercise
Martini:	an 'Italian fortified wine flavoured with herbs
groundsman's roller:	the heavy cylindrical machine used to flatten the cricket pitch by the man who keeps the pitch in good condition
pavilion:	the building with seating, bars and dressing-rooms at a cricket ground
cisterns:	water tanks
bungalows and villas:	typical one- and two-storeyed houses in suburban Britain
rapists:	people intending sexual violence against women

'Horses in a Suburban Field'

It is not specified what kind of horses Douglas Dunn is describing – race horses, cart-horses, ponies – but they are out of any context that would seem natural to them.

COMMENTARY:

A suburban area is neither rural nor citified. Cities have not usually developed in a methodical way but have gradually, spasmodically encroached on the surrounding countryside, and what were farms, woods, open areas, small villages have been incorporated into housing estates, industrial areas, parks, shopping centres, transport networks. There are still small fields and part of an aristocratic country estate, but any sense of open freedom, freshness and style has gone. The city is spilling out on to what was there, and it is significant that the poem begins and ends with dust, the debris of urbanisation. The poem moves through a reiteration of dulled elements: 'Discarded things rot', 'rust', 'dried-up', 'dead dreams'. Dunn does not introduce the horses till the second section, after the first section has established an atmosphere of displacement and decline. The boundary hedges now seem to 'enclose' the fields in a constricting way and the grand planned estate with its arranged trees has had to be forfeited. Even the children playing in the long grass seem to have been sent there to be 'Out of the way' and to give some relief to their parents; it is not clear whose headache is soothed. The horses appear diminished, 'Sad and captured', in such polluted surroundings. Normally, horses have a steady gaze; in the 'towny field' they can only 'peep', they cannot gallop but 'step' and 'wander' through the rubbish. The dust in the second from last line represents the 'dead dreams' of housewives who, sad and captured like the horses, seem to have lost all vitality, and aspirations to a better life. It may be that 'the dead dreams' are actually the horses who had known freedom before their present dulled lives and, in that respect, are symbolic of the housewives, with their bleak domestic chores.

In appearance the poem approximates to a traditional sonnet, with a pause between its octave and its sestet. On closer examination, it is too long to be a fourteen-line sonnet and, although the lines look of similar length to each other, there is no strict regularity and no rhyme scheme. Perhaps like the suburban field it is almost something definite but, in fact, it is neither open country nor exactly planned town.

NOTES AND GLOSSARY:
noblemen: aristocrats of an earlier period who owned the land
death duty: a state tax to be paid on property inherited at someone's death
towny: of the town (as distinct from of the country); some-

| | times used pejoratively to describe the superficial and somewhat impractical style which town-dwellers are said to adopt |
| **hawthorn:** | smallish thorny tree with pink or white blossom and red berries, common throughout Britain; also called 'may' |

'Ships'

The poem pictures cargo ships setting off, probably for some foreign country, and imagines the thoughts of the unemployed young men who remain in the towns near the mouth of the river.

COMMENTARY:

In his first book of poems Douglas Dunn has only two poems specifically set in his native Scotland. They are both located in the Clyde Estuary, near where Dunn was brought up; this poem is one of them. The area was the main British centre of ship-building, marine engineering, and the training ground for skilled seamen. A vast network of employment and wealth depended on the marine activity which had contributed to make Glasgow the second city (after London) of the British Empire in the period up to the Second World War. In the 1950s and 1960s a massive decline took place in ship-building and heavy engineering; the poem emerges from this change in circumstances.

Ships leaving port at night, usually because of the tide, are full of mystery. Where are they going? What are they carrying? Will they return? Dunn touches on this mysterious quality by juxtaposing a ship with swans. The creatures of the natural world gaze uncomprehendingly at the man-made things: the ships, the lights, the houses, the machinery. The natural world is altered by the human activity; oil pollutes the birds, new waves are made by ships' propellers. The local rain momentarily coats the departing ship but will dry off without trace. The cosmopolitan nature of the crews on many cargo ships brings together people who have totally different loyalties and aspirations. The ordinary seamen recruited from the Far East have no local attachments and play cards to occupy their time off duty; the officer from Scotland thinks of what he is leaving behind. In the generations before, male members of families near the river made their living and sacrificed their lives for their country as seamen. The youths, unemployed now that war is over and the shipyards and shipping are no longer needed, ponder over what took place in the past and what does not happen now. The futility of their wishes and resolutions is conveyed by Dunn in the 'thousand times' and 'their empty hands'. All around them are reminders of the old reliable bond with ships and the bleakness of their present lives. Dunn encapsulates a huge social change and its human costs in a neat arrangement of images which comment on each other.

NOTES AND GLOSSARY:

Clyde: a river in Scotland flowing through Glasgow. Its shipyards were responsible for some of the biggest liners and many other ships

hill-climbing houses: houses built on the slopes leading away from the river. Some of the houses are very grand, and 'climbing' may suggest their social aspirations

malefic cranes: the tall machinery for lifting heavy objects in the docks has a sinister or evil appearance looming out of the dark sky

Lascars: poorly paid seamen from various parts of the Far East, particularly India

mate: an officer on a ship next in authority to the captain

Ayrshire: a county to the south of the Clyde

clubfooted peninsulas: some of the headlands and stretches of land sticking out into the sea to the north of the Clyde estuary are shaped like elongated lumps or clubs. 'Clubfooted' suggests misshapen awkwardness

river towns: towns such as Clydebank, Port Glasgow and Greenock

ringed: a circle has been drawn round them in the photographs to distinguish them

complements: crews

model destroyers: hand-made models of destroyers, ships designed to destroy torpedo-boats

glass cafés: fashion at the time favoured the lavish use of glass and mirrors

American soft drinks: a new fashion (which suggested that America was the smart place to be)

Poems from *The Happier Life* (1972)

Fewer than half of the poems in this collection are included in *Selected Poems 1964–1983*. Several differences are apparent between *Terry Street* and *The Happier Life*. In the former, no poem is longer than a page and a half; in the latter, there are nine poems longer than this, five of them being twice as long. Rhyme was not used in the earlier collection whereas half a dozen poems, mostly the longer ones, in *The Happier Life* use consistent rhyme schemes. Humour is more obvious and more benevolent in the latter volume, and the poet takes more pleasure in more situations. Several poems are based on autobiographical material and locate Dunn's background in a wider historical context. The range of subjects and moods is wider, with some very light verse and some very stern or solemn poems. Dunn's awareness of himself as a poet is now more accepted in the poems, and several deal with his views on his art. He speaks more clearly on behalf of areas of British society dismissed as insignificant by the power-centres of the nation. His observation of the inhabitants of Terry Street has been extended to include more kinds of people, sometimes seen as veiled aspects of himself, sometimes of interest because they are so different from himself.

'Backwaters'

The poem describes three different kinds of place where different kinds of people have their existence. The centre of Dunn's attention is the 'backwaters', the places of no obvious importance in national or international affairs.

COMMENTARY:
Dunn uses the term 'places' with deliberation; he does not mean towns, although some towns would fit the label, but the apparent vagueness of 'places' points to a mode of living wherever it might happen. The opening stanza introduces us to the particular places on which he will concentrate in the final four stanzas; in stanzas 2–6 he describes two different kinds of places which stand as contrasts to the backwater. The places he looks at in stanzas 2 and 3, are centres of entertainment and commerce, destinations of travel, and the hub of the country's activities. However, Dunn's description is not expressed in neutral terms; there is something cheap and self-centred and cynical associated with such places. The 'signed photographs' and 'sharp suits' manifest a shallowness, and the public are seen as 'mugs' to be deceived. The second places he describes, in stanzas 4–6, seem to those who live there, comfortable, natural, entirely what they expect. In such places it is easy to believe that all people everywhere live in a very similar way, or that places elsewhere can be judged by the essential normality represented by such places. The third kind of place does not enjoy the easy acceptance of the first two kinds. It is disregarded or pointedly ignored by the knowing inhabitants of the first and second places and its own inhabitants feel no sense of belonging or importance. It is as if they have slid into an anonymity where people from the other places can no longer see them. Nonetheless, such places and their inhabitants represent an aspect of society which exists on the edge of cultivated assumptions and which most of us do not wish to acknowledge, like 'the bad days in our lives'. Dunn presents such places in terms of disabilities and deformities (lines 23 and 24), and the sufferers gape in servile amazement at any show of glamour or power. In the bleak final stanza he states more explicitly that these places, these people, are not some tidy category of the poor or lower class which we, the lucky or complacent ones, can decide to ignore; 'they are permanent' and represent an aspect of the lives of

all of us. Behind the glitter of entertainers and commerce, beneath the securities of a good neighbourhood, lie a frightening dullness and fear and inadequacy.

In the thirty lines of the poem there occur over forty plural nouns, relentlessly emphasising the generality of the condition seen by Dunn and just as relentlessly removing any possibility of individual response. And yet there is a sympathy for the helplessness and the emptiness at the centre of our lives, the 'permanent' condition of our being.

NOTES AND GLOSSARY:

Backwaters: stretches of water attached to a river but removed from the main stream; used metaphorically for stagnant situations where nothing of significance or freshness occurs

dilapidated: decayed, in a state of disrepair

with distinct pejorative overtones: critically or dismissively, with a clearly implied superiority on the part of the speakers

Comedians and singers: nationally known entertainers (on a tour of major centres)

sharp: fashionable in a rather obvious or vulgar way (with a suggestion of a deceiving appearance and lack of honesty)

paradise of transactions: a salesman's dream situation where miraculously profitable business deals can be arranged

mugs: members of the public who can be seduced into buying by the advertising

civilian: urbane, civilised, removed from any hint of war and armies

kind insignia: uniform badges indicating their helpfulness

pensioned: beyond employment, paid-off

at the far end of all achievements: beyond hope of ever achieving anything

kiln-baked: constructed of bricks made in an oven (suggesting a walled-in, impersonal, unchanging condition)

they are permanent: this perhaps recalls the words of Jesus in the Bible: 'For the poor always ye have with you' (John 12:5)

'After the War'

Set in the period immediately after the Second World War, the poem gives a strong impression of being based on an incident in Dunn's own boyhood. The overlap between a real war with real soldiers and the games of young boys is forcefully realised, and there are details, such as the broken egg and the family without a father, which convey the intimacy of personal experience.

COMMENTARY:

Any poem written by an adult about a childhood experience will contain a mixture of adult elements and childish ones. In this case, Douglas Dunn writes reminiscently and makes no attempt to express directly a child's way of comprehending a situation: for example, phrases such as 'blue shards of an egg' and 'abrasive loss' issue from an educated adult's vocabulary and consciousness. However, the whole mystery of soldiers, war and death, and the sense of bafflement in the poem are strongly indicative of a child's innocence and partial understanding of experience. The incident is described, for the most part, as happening to a group of boys but the significance of it for Dunn is marked by the three personal perceptions in lines 10, 23 and 24. The boy, in the midst of play, sensed something of destruction, separation and loss and, looking back across the poem, we can trace a trail of emotional markers from the callously broken egg, the bleeding faces of fathers, the faces of dead children, to the dereliction of the final half dozen lines and the emphasis of 'alone', 'untended', 'broken', 'abrasive loss', 'creaked' and 'rusted'. As the poem develops, the gap between playing at soldiers and the actuality of death emerges, but the ending is quiet, unexplicit, even somewhat enigmatic. It is the cumulative effect of hints and directions, and not any categorical statement, that allows us to conclude that the other boy's father has been killed in the war. We come to discern the human story behind the excitement of soldiers and badges and games in a manner similar to the way the boys glimpse something of the ordinary humanness of the soldiers in uniform who 'brewed tea in Snoddy's field' and 'pee/In Snoddy's stagnant pond'. Elements of innocence and play come to carry heavier meanings: pine cones can be seen as little hand grenades and plimsolls on fallen blossom can suggest army boots on the 'faces of dead children'. For the fatherless boy the reminders are too painful. The three short sentences in the poem (lines 10, 23 and 29) have an arresting quality in their very brevity and mark the stages of the poem's drama.

NOTES AND GLOSSARY:

Snoddy:	a local farmer (Snoddy is a Scottish name)
select:	particular
skirmishers:	fighters in short or lighter actions, like guerrilla fighters
shards:	fragments (often used of broken pottery)
Browning:	automatic pistol
badges:	buttons and badges from army uniforms showing the rank or regiment of a soldier were highly prized by young boys who often made collections of them
plimsolls:	light canvas rubber-soled sports shoes, gym shoes
May-blossom:	flowers of the hawthorn tree (which commonly blooms in the month of May)

an untended garden: indicating the absence of a man in the house
abrasive: wearing one down in a painful way, wounding

'Guerrillas'

Set in a village of suburban childhood, the poem explores emotions of inferiority, rivalry, envy and revenge.

COMMENTARY:
This poem could be easily misinterpreted as being concerned with the seemingly perennial British subject of class. However, class, in the sense of upper, middle and lower classes in society, is not what the poem is about. There are various details such as the daffodils and 'the awkward wire' that point to a personal memory on Dunn's part although the experience described would be shared by many children living in a community such as a small country town. The children from the surrounding farms may often feel that the children living in the town have a sophistication and network of friends which they themselves do not have. Equally, the town children, even when they see the farm children as somewhat unrefined, look at them with a sense that they belong more firmly to where they come from and are real owners of the land on which they live, whereas they, the town people, are more like temporary tenants. This sense has, indeed, to do with a relationship of the country children to the earth and the things of nature. It is as if the town children required the permission of the others to be allowed to perform the simplest action in the countryside. The casual power wielded by the country children extends even to the teachers, or so the town children believe, and this power generates a mystery which includes their 'dangerous dogs and stately horses'. The town boys come to see themselves as intruders or raiders ('guerrillas') who try to sabotage this power (lines 14–15). Their actions are petty, futile and motivated by envy. In the final two lines Dunn gives an added depth to their feelings for revenge by suggesting that they partake of an inherited humiliation, that their forebears had been dispossessed. Perhaps the 'as if' in the second last line indicates that the idea is a way of rationalising our giving way so easily to emotions of which we publicly disapprove.

NOTES AND GLOSSARY:
Guerrillas: fighters who attack a bigger force in indirect or unsustained ways to try to wear down the enemy
free eggs: given as gifts. (It is possible that Dunn is looking back to his own childhood; eggs were rationed for some years after the Second World War and were difficult to obtain)

awkward wire:	boundary fence, possibly of barbed wire, through which it is difficult to climb
bad words:	insults, swearwords
froggy drains:	drains where frogs bred
a hand:	the hand of a murderer

Poems from *Love or Nothing* (1974)

About half of the poems in this collection are included in *Selected Poems 1964–1983*. There is a strong impression of experiment in this volume: experiment in form, subject matter, shifts in tone and poetic personae. As in the first two collections Dunn tends to write in stanzas of a regular length and, as in *The Happier Life*, about half a dozen poems use consistent rhyme patterns. Many of the pieces have a concern with situations of uncertainty, and he experiments with writing from the viewpoint of a person other than himself. Sometimes the mood is ironic and self-conscious, reminiscent at times of T. S. Eliot's character, Prufrock. Dunn extends his exploration of his childhood and Scottish background, but often it would be difficult to ascertain his national or social orientation. A surreal element is present, and the juxtaposition of images is very demanding. Often it seems that the physical world around him does not correspond to the emotional world within him, and a reiterated effect of the collection is one of awkwardness and disconnection.

'Renfrewshire Traveller'

The poem explores the feelings of the poet returning to the area where he grew up, and raises questions about such a return.

COMMENTARY:

Most modern Scottish poets at some time in their careers write a poem about coming back to Scotland after an absence. Emigration, exile, separation, homesickness, bitterness at removal – all these are common subjects in Scottish writing. Living elsewhere creates alterations in accent, tastes, perspectives, and to return after some years can bring accusations of disloyalty and pretentiousness from the people among whom one grew up. There are other questions. Will the people back home still recognise the wanderer, and will he or she recognise the people and place they left behind?

In the poem there are two direct questions: 'Have I come back?' (twice) and 'What have I come to?' The first question can be read in different ways according to where the reader places the emphasis: '*Have* I come back?' or 'Have *I* come back?' or 'Have I come *back*?' Even the second question is not entirely straightforward. Is the question about himself and where he is in life? or is he enquiring about the place to which he has returned? These ambiguities are indicative of an uncertainty running through the whole poem from the odd, confusing image in the opening line: 'Home rain, an aerial night-Clyde'. The hyphen joins together the notions of darkness and the river, and the combination stands for the gloomy rain in the sky. Equally, as the sky and the earth are indistinguishable, the past ('recollection') is fused with the present ('welcome'). In the obscuring darkness and rain even the familiar landmarks seem somewhat unreliable. The train north towards Glasgow goes through Kilmarnock, home of the best-selling whisky in the world. The sign for Johnny Walker bears its trademark, a gentleman wearing a monocle which catches the light intermittently and, hence, appears to blink. In this third stanza Dunn squashes together three items: the image and two resulting thoughts. From the viewpoint of Johnny Walker, history and the world at large is seen in terms of whisky, a viewpoint shared by the town which relies heavily on its largest employer and the product. This limited and gloomy view of life is like the Roman apprehension that, behind all our grandiose actions, the human condition is one of tears and sadness.

In his awkward self-awareness the poet insists on his Scottishness but, living in England, he sometimes appears as quaintly or stereotypically Scottish and out of place there too. His Scottishness is decomposing out of its native context, and he feels stranger each time he returns. The main obligation to return is the death of relatives, and when they are gone there may be no force left to pull him back. He no longer knows how, or even if, he is connected to this home ground in the West of Scotland; nothing of it is distinct in the dark and rain, where he hears old accents and sees blurred buildings. And yet it remains, in some sense, where he came from, part of him.

NOTES AND GLOSSARY:

Renfrewshire: a county in Scotland immediately south-west of the city of Glasgow. Dunn was born in Renfrewshire

Home rain: the west of Scotland has a much higher rainfall than Hull in the east of England where Dunn was living at this time

Kilmarnock: a large town in Ayrshire, twenty-five miles south-west of Glasgow

lacrimae rerum: part of a quotation from the *Aeneid* by the Latin poet Virgil (70–19BC). The whole line reads: 'Sunt lacrimae rerum et mentem mortalia tangunt' ('There are tears of pity for the nature of things, and human mortality touches the heart'). The phrase *lacrimae rerum* has come to mean the sadness underlying human achievement

tartan ... shortbread: these rich crumbly biscuits are a Scottish speciality and are often sold in tartan-patterned tin boxes

delicatessen: a shop selling exclusive or exotic foods

afright: panic (usually spelt 'affright')

brilliant ... butter: the base of the buildings cannot be seen in the bright wetness but their glistening shapes emerge higher up, blurred by the rain

'The Competition'

Based on a chance encounter on a bus when he was ten, the poem charts Dunn's awakening to an awareness of class differences and the otherness of people. It stands as a companion piece to the poem 'Boys With Coats'.

COMMENTARY:

A wry, even ironic, tone emerges in this piece of reminiscence as Dunn recalls his earnestness as a young boy. The title, 'The Competition', operates in several ways throughout the poem but certainly it relates to the way in which people, and particularly children, assess themselves by comparing their position with that of other people. Two incidents are described and the second is used to comment on the first. The poem opens in the socially neutral territory of a public bus, and the boy in the seat in front attracts the young Dunn's attention for two reasons. First, he is seen as alike in that he has a model aeroplane 'just like mine'. Secondly, however, he is seen as utterly unlike because of the school uniform he is wearing which is an odd colour and which represents a private school, thereby marking him out as rich and/or of a different social class. The substantial detour, detailing the colour of the uniform and its associations for the young Dunn, acts as a balancing device, keeping the other boy under control. As a boy of ten, Dunn can see only that he and the boy have something in common, a toy aeroplane, but the boy's mother is horrified at the attempted contact as if she fears her son may be contaminated. Being rebuffed by the boy and his mother deeply upsets him, and eventually his grandfather has to try to cheer him up with money; there is a 'consolation' in feeling more hurt than anyone else and in believing that only he could be given a sixpence by his grandfather.

His sense of resentment has lingered on, and the second incident delivers a little rebuke to his harboured grudge. Forced to run barefoot and, therefore, looking very much 'a poor boy', he imagines, rightly or wrongly we do not know, that the other boy is his main rival in a long race. With his resentment pushing him on, he urges himself to his limits, only to be beaten at the very end of the race, not by someone socially superior, but by a boy lower in the social scale than himself.

Although the poem is written by Dunn as an adult, the process by which a young person arrives at a concept such as 'class' is convincingly rooted in something personal and disproportionate to the concept. The disproportionate attention given in lines 6–10 to dung is also typical of the fascination with such matters at a certain age. The lines of verse have an approximate consistency of length and number of stresses but the impression given is of unhurried, unforced reminiscence. At the conclusion, the five words making up the name of the club require a deliberate, careful articulation and achieve an effect of a pronounced, final statement.

NOTES AND GLOSSARY:

Hamilton:	a town south of Glasgow
Leyland:	the name of a manufacturer of buses and cars
named for Eddlewood:	the destination is a district of Hamilton
Zoomed:	imitated the movements of a plane
Cousar's coup:	the dung-heap of a local farmer
fee-paying places:	private schools (sometimes called public schools in England)
blue-bottled byre:	a cowshed full of large flies
Hurricane:	a famous British fighter aeroplane during the Second World War
sixpence:	a reasonable reward for a child in 1952
trained . . . to ruin:	worn out my spiked running shoes
weathers:	extremes
Shotts . . . Club:	an athletic club attached to a nearby coal-mine

Poems from *Barbarians* (1979)

Three quarters of the poems in this collection are included in *Selected Poems 1964–1983*. The original collection is in three sections: I, 'Barbarian Pastorals', and II and III which are untitled. Half of the poems use regular rhyme.

The nine 'Barbarian Pastorals' develop the socio-political side of Dunn's thinking so evident in his early work in *Terry Street*. Varieties of challenge to societal orthodoxy are explored in different contexts and different times: present-day England; first-century Rome; rural England in 1789, the year of the French Revolution; Scotland in 1820, a time of political turmoil; contemporary America; the artist in relation to a patron. Many of the poems throughout the collection are concerned with the shifting boundary lines between groups of people and attitudes. Points of transition in modes of living are focused on, whether the point be someone retiring from work, growing from childhood to adulthood, an alteration in a relationship, or even death. The epigraph from Paul Nizan which prefaces the volume obviously voices a question which vexes Dunn and,

throughout these poems, there is a recurring worry about personal integrity
in changing circumstances. A very positive development from much of his
earlier work is a new openness in dealing with emotion: sorrow, loss,
pleasure, love, regret, confusion are all faced more directly in *Barbarians*
and written about, not in comforting terms, but without the edgy disguises
and obliquity so characteristic of the earlier collections.

'In the Grounds'

In the original collection this is the second poem in the group called
'Barbarian Pastorals' and it has a subtitle, 'Yorkshire, 1975', which locates
it specifically. It presents a confrontation between the wealthy gentility of
a land-owning class and the awkward feelings of people who are deemed
to intrude on this exclusive world. The poem should be read in conjunction
with the neighbouring poems as far as 'The Wealth'.

COMMENTARY:
One of the most obvious features of this poem is the formality of its verse,
syntax and vocabulary. The lines regularly contain ten syllables, usually
with five main stresses, and the rhyme scheme is totally consistent and
tight. The structure of sentences is sophisticated and demands a fastidious
care in the reader; try, for example, stanzas 1 and 4. In its vocabulary
and turns of phrase the poem is often graceful and gracious in a
way reminiscent of some seventeenth-century poets, particularly Andrew
Marvell. Marvell, too, was fond of contemplating conflicts and com-
promises between the cultivated and the wild. Dunn introduces himself as
one of the people labelled as barbarians, the rabble, but he writes in a
highly cultivated manner showing an intimacy with history and linguistic
stylishness. This discrepancy between the label put on him and his
sophistication demolishes the force of class discrimination. The final two
stanzas present the land-owners' fear of the intruders in the extravagant
images of the rich order of the Chinese Empire being pillaged by savage
Mongol hordes.

There are basic differences between the land-inheriting, established
class and Dunn and his socialist friends who are 'intransigent, at odds with
them', but he claims that some pleasures can be shared, particularly a
delight in nature and gardens:

We walk as people on the paths of gods
And in our minds we harmonize them both.

The protected world of country houses and landscaped grounds cannot
tolerate any suggestion of change or sharing: the privileged circle will be
broken and vulgar anarchy will rush in. Although the subtitle and details
of the description make the poem seem realistic and based on an actual

incident, the enclosed estate with its 'pretty world' is symbolic of a wider division and suspicion in English society. It appears that the barbarians are betrayed by their accents (line 3), that is, they are from the working class or from outside England and, in their accents, remain 'true/To who we are'. Although, in stanza 4, the mood of the intruders disclaims any revolutionary intention, in the apprehensive eyes of the upper class they constitute a threat to all stability.

NOTES AND GLOSSARY:

'In the Grounds':	'grounds' is the term used to describe the enclosed, often extensive, landscaped area of land around a large house
Barbarians:	uncivilised or brutal people. (The original Greek word may have derived from Greeks mocking the speech of non-Greeks as meaningless 'bar-bar bar-bar')
rose:	the emblematic flower of English gardens and of England and, indirectly, of a cultivated way of life
paths of gods:	the shapes of nature (perhaps a lightly mocking description of the grandiose planning in the estate)
Disclosures:	revelations, views, and also unexpected vistas
Irish wolfhounds:	very large, rough-coated dogs used in hunting or as guard dogs
parterre:	formally patterned flower garden, with gravelled paths (hence the noise of their boots on the gravel)
intransigent:	unwilling to compromise
rabble-dreams:	ideas that working class people should have more power; socialism
England's . . . leaf:	the English aristocratic tradition of large country houses and elaborate gardens
unkempt:	untidy, referring particularly to uncombed hair
we hurt . . . truth:	the truth of the privileged that their estate is lovely is challenged by the barbarians' truth that such loveliness can be available to anyone irrespective of class
Drool:	dribble, slobber
ale-stinking hair:	various 'barbarians' have been presented as drunken, dirty and wild-haired
mandarins:	the name given by Europeans to high-ranking, cultured officials of the Chinese Empire; used here to mean the rulers in China at the time of the Mongol invasions in the thirteenth century
hawk:	sell in the streets, going from house to house
plate:	silver cutlery and serving-dishes
saddle-kings:	chiefs of the nomadic Mongols

'Portrait Photograph, 1915'

The poem is spoken by a man who was killed in the First World War and who survives in a photograph. Part of the point of the poem is to insist that a person's worth is not calculable merely in terms of the number of photographs taken of him or her or in some public acclaim.

COMMENTARY:
The eighteen lines form one single sentence and the absence of stops and gaps emphasises a sense of continuity and inter-connectedness. The poem is a musing reminiscence but for the most part of a generalised sort: 'multitudes', 'newsreel beyond newsreel', 'troopships', 'descendants'. One incident stands out, indicated by 'once' (line 7) and 'it was my turn' (line 10), when the speaker's individual photograph was taken. The title carries a declarative force: 'Portrait Photograph, 1915'. The word 'portrait' suggests someone famous who poses for an artist to eternalise him or her in a picture. The portrait in the poem, however, is created mechanically, and the subject is merely one person in a long queue. Nonetheless, for the man concerned, it is a special occasion, and the date fixes something of its significance: he is about to set off to fight and die in the war. The photograph lifts him out of anonymity and gives him a notion of permanence, of 'posterity'.

The direction of thought in the poem is indicated in the word 'too' in the opening line. Usually the individual photographs, the portraits, were of the officers, the commanding figures, but Dunn, through the ordinary soldier, insists: 'We too have our place', we who are ordinarily observed only in crowd scenes. The huge death toll in the trench warfare in northern France deprived individual soldiers of any significance. Is human dignity printed on a posed photograph, 'Fading a little', strong enough to stand against the obliteration of the war? Is the opening claim, 'We too have our place', denied by the rest of the poem?

NOTES AND GLOSSARY:
Rising . . . smoke: a description of futile attacks from the trenches
pipers: bag-pipers playing the troops on to the ships which will carry them to France
Anderson's . . . Salon: a rather grandiose name for a photographer's shop, probably in Glasgow
posterity: future generations
her: his wife's

Poems from *St Kilda's Parliament* (1981)

Of the thirty-three poems in the original collection only five are not included in *Selected Poems 1964–1983*. This is the fullest representation of all the collections included, and the fact indicates Dunn's own high regard for the volume.

The book is dedicated to the poet's father who died in 1980 and, sentiment apart, the dedication is appropriate to the contents in that a substantial proportion of the poems are concerned with widening and deepening Dunn's understanding of a Scottish tradition to which he belongs by birth and upbringing. Several of the longer and most rewarding poems investigate how Scottish writers of earlier periods related to prevailing social conditions in which the writer was not considered as very important. In these poems, too, Dunn displays a sharp interest in the linguistic expression of a community; this is the only one of his collections to include a glossary of Scots words used in half a dozen poems. Despite or because of their localised setting, the poems comprehend a wider range of thoughts and emotions than are to be encountered in the earlier volumes.

His earlier experiments in poems written in the voice of a devised character are extended into what he calls 'poem-films' starring such actor-types as Anthony Quinn and Jean-Paul Belmondo. These experiments are less successful than either his reconstructions of situations in earlier periods, for example, 'St Kilda's Parliament' and 'Green Breeks', or his playful inflations of the ordinary, for example, 'Ode to a Paperclip' and 'Ratatouille'.

'St Kilda's Parliament: 1879–1979'

The poem imagines a photographer returning to the remote island he had photographed one hundred years earlier. Half way between his first visit and this imagined one, the inhabitants of the island were all evacuated. The poem enquires into the lives of the islanders and our attitude to them as observers. Can we learn something by looking at the story of this isolated community?

COMMENTARY:

The story of St Kilda is unusually fascinating. This island or group of islands, situated in the Atlantic one hundred and ten miles west of the Scottish mainland, supported a population of about a hundred for centuries. The people survived at a frugal level on a diet based mainly on sea birds and their eggs. The islands have almost no arable land and consist of wind-swept cliffs rising sheer from the ocean, the home of hundreds of thousands of sea birds. Themselves subject to diseases and natural disasters, the inhabitants for long stretches of time knew nothing of the wars, fashions and technical developments in the rest of the world. By 1930 the population had dropped to an unviable thirty-six, and poverty and illness forced them to request that they be evacuated to the mainland. By that time also they had become objects of tourist curiosity, and their way of life could not have survived.

Dunn's poem is based on a famous photograph of the men of the community taken in the final quarter of the nineteenth century and on various accounts written about the islanders. His fascination is with people whose conditions of living and terms of reference are so different from our assumptions that they challenge our central notions of what we mean by human, social and natural. How do they see us? The poem opens with a reading of what is shown in the photograph. At that date the St Kildans had no understanding of a camera or even of the photographer – he could not speak their language. The 'set half-smile' on their faces is enigmatic but seems to Dunn to derive from the otherness of their lives. In lines 22–32 he develops this view of their difference from mainlanders such as the photographer and describes them as products of their wild circumstances.

In the second section the photographer-narrator attributes to the St Kildans a knowledge – 'Look at their sly, assuring mockery' – and a confidence in what they are that contrasts with the disintegrated, 'civilised' world portrayed in his photographs (lines 80–84). Despite the fact that their culture eventually succumbed to the pressures of the commercial modern world, he sees a solidity, a rootedness in their communal subsistence on their island. The poem ends with an unanswered question as to whether, all those years ago, when he took the photograph, they looked at him and the world he represented with acceptance or rejection, 'Benevolent, or malign?' The poem in its long capacious sentences meandering through the unmechanical, unrhymed pentameters of the lines raises large questions about values: about community and individuality, about how different groups from different cultures see each other, what is given helpfully and what is given destructively, what we can understand in what we see. The central image of the photograph fixes the St Kildans at a particular point in a particular pose, but is the camera able to see behind the 'set half-smile'?

NOTES AND GLOSSARY:

St Kilda's Parliament: the title given to a photograph taken in about 1879 by G. W. Wilson of the men of the island meeting, as they did each week-day morning, to plan the work for the day and to discuss any matter of communal interest. There was no leader, and each adult male had a chance to speak and an equal vote in decisions. The photograph can be seen in most books on St Kilda

files: rows (they stand facing each other in the narrow space between the houses)

tam-o'-shanter: a Scottish soft woollen brimless bonnet with a

solan goose: pom-pom on top, commonly worn in the nineteenth century

 a gannet; a large, strong-winged sea-bird, caught in large numbers by the men on the cliffs, and used as food

dulse ... sea-tangle: edible varieties of seaweed

pig ... rabbit: these creatures were not found or known about on St Kilda

carpentry ... waters: in the Hebrides boats were the main form of transport, and generations of experience determined the best designs for the conditions. There were no secure harbours on St Kilda

Hebrides: the islands off the west coast of Scotland. St Kilda is about fifty miles beyond any of the populated Hebridean islands

depopulation: this occurred in 1930 when the islanders were evacuated. (The island is now owned by the National Trust for Scotland but is also used by the Ministry of Defence as a rocket-tracking station)

archaeology ... lichen: the history of the island will have layers of natural growth ('hazelraw' is Scots for 'lichen') and of human traces now covered by the lichen

toes ... boulder: in the photograph many of the men are bare-footed, and one is standing on a large stone

manacles: imprisoning chains

Romantic Staffas: Staffa is an island in the Inner Hebrides, famous and much visited from the end of the eighteenth century for its fantastic rock formations. Poets, artists and composers (for example, Mendelssohn) were inspired by it

Gaelic: the Celtic language spoken in north-west Scotland and the Hebrides

Hierarchies ... literacy: fancy food and book education which make people compare themselves with others

This flick ... shuttered: this moment I caught in a photograph

Casual husbandry: a subsistence economy was accepted by the islanders as their way of life

St Kilda ... wren: a species unique to the island

Ornithological: studying the varieties and behaviour of birds

Zulu massacres: British troops and Zulu tribesmen in south-east Africa fought each other in 1879

Tchaikovsky's opera: *Eugene Onegin* by the Russian composer Piotr Ilyich Tchaikovsky, first performed in Moscow in 1879

elegants:	fashionable people
commercial copulations:	pornographic photographs
larger franchise:	freedom to travel in the wider world
whittle time:	pass time idly (like paring down a piece of wood with a knife)

'Witch-Girl'

Dunn describes how the mother of a malformed girl is burned to death as a witch and how the daughter wanders round Scotland. Something of the girl seems to survive into the present day and the poem investigates what this represents.

COMMENTARY:

In 1727 Janet Horne was arrested at Dornoch in north-east Scotland and accused of witchcraft. If was claimed that her daughter, whose hands were misshapen with an abnormal amount of nail, was a creature of the Devil and that her mother rode on her as on a horse to covens (meetings of witches). Whether the girl escaped or was released is not known but Janet Horne who was old, frail and probably senile was condemned to death. She was stripped, covered in tar and carried around the town. It was a bitterly cold day and the old woman, led to the bonfire, tried to warm her hands before she was thrown into the flames. This true story is the basis of Dunn's poem.

'Witch-girl' in nine evenly paced, regularly rhyming stanzas is a story with a twist of ideas right at the end. Each stanza advances the story and the quiet regularity seems to defuse the grotesque elements and make the incident less remarkable. The whole affair is also distanced by the use of reportage: 'they said' . . . 'They spoke'. Certainly the gruesome details carry their own fascination but Dunn's interest is not in exploiting the sensational aspects. Rather, he is concerned with a question which emerges from the story and particularly from the girl's share of it. In the final stanza the shift from past to present tense – 'If she is dead' . . . 'I see her' . . . 'And hear her breathing' – forces the reader to re-read the poem with a new urgency. If she is *not* dead, where is she and what is she? Throughout the poem, she is identified with the natural world of weather, plants and animals. First she is seen as a horse, then, in stanza 5, as a bird and, in stanza 6, as a beast. In stanza 6 she bathes in rivers across the whole country and, in the final stanza, she is again associated with rivers. The flowers she tries to sell are seen as part of her and her unhappiness is shared by the 'earth and animals within her'. Somehow, in Dunn's mind, she is still present in the twentieth century but not in human things – 'she is breathing in the wood and stone'. For him, she represents something which persists and is still denied by the narrow-minded Scottish mentality.

Anything unusual or eccentric has to be hounded out of orthodox society and the strongest weapon of the orthodox is religious condemnation. In stanzas 2–4 the people, mainly men, are described in a peculiar mixture of religious terms ('pious', 'presbyters', 'fear of God', 'psalmed') and animal terms ('giddy-ups', 'whinnied, neighed,/Clip-clopped'). It is as if they have more in common with her than they wish to concede and, in killing the old woman as a witch, they could destroy the devil in themselves. However, if the girl is devilish she is gentle and harmless while they are filled with hate and violence; some do pity the mother (line 12) but they do not prevent the burning. Dunn feels that in Scotland a harsh religion has served to shut out the imaginative and gentler side of humanity and promote a mechanical, forbidding mentality. This denial of what used to be described as the feminine side of human nature continues in our time, hence the present tense in the final stanza.

NOTES AND GLOSSARY:

lightless:	of darkness
spelled:	enchanted, transformed
Sutherland:	a county in the extreme north of Scotland
Law:	the authorities, whether legal or not
giddy-ups:	commands to a horse to move on
Tolbooth:	the town gaol (with straw on the floor)
presbyters:	officials or elders in the Presbyterian church
Dornoch:	a town in Sutherland
psalmed:	sang psalms, hymns derived from the Bible
Oykell . . . Forth:	rivers in the north and south of Scotland
spurned:	rejected with contempt
barbed:	made painful
hawked:	sold in the streets
Trongate:	an area of Glasgow with a market
braziers:	night fires set in metal baskets
City Guard:	an early form of police force
Gryfe . . . Tay:	rivers in various parts of Scotland

'Washing the Coins'

Earning one's wages is a memorable event. The poem recalls the crushing hardness of the boy's work in a potato field and the wonderful revelation and reward of seeing clearly his first earnings.

COMMENTARY:

This is a poem of evocation and vivid detail rather than a venture into big ideas. Not that these two categories have to be rigidly separate, but particular poems do tend to take a predominant direction. Although the many specificities indicate a personal experience, Dunn generalises the experience by his use of 'you' ('You'd start at seven') down to line 37 when we encounter the first 'I'; it is as if we could all share the mundane aspects of work but he remembers a twist unique to himself. In the first part of the poem the emphasis is very heavily on physical sensations, and the only emotions are of pain and resentment. There are hardly any larger perspectives or releases from the unrelenting toil. Even 'a glance upwards' gives no relief; the sky seems to collude with the heavy ground; and the scene shows people in a miserable servitude. Through this grinding description of the day's work, however, the boy is shown learning about his abilities and weaknesses, in relation to the more experienced Irish workers, to the limits of his own endurance, till he reaches an awareness, first, that 'It was the same for everyone' and then:

> Towards the end you felt you understood
> The happy rancour of the Irish howkers.

This initiation into knowing himself and also learning that, in many respects, he is indistinguishable from other people is encapsulated in the incident where the farmer's wife, who knows him as a neighbour, cannot immediately recognise him because of the mud caked on his face.

Her payment of him is like a blessing, a special acceptance, and connects with the concluding revelation in the final lines. Line 45, however, seems out of place and unclear. Standing as a complete sentence, it appears to be a large statement but what does it say? Does it mean that the boy is so tired that he cannot look beyond the present? Or does it mean that the boy senses, because of the warmth of the farmer's wife, a continuity of community and that it would be very unpleasant not to feel such a thing? The fact that Dunn entitles the poem 'Washing the Coins' draws attention to and gives centrality to the final part of the poem. The cleaned coins of his wages in the clear water of the basin achieve a heraldic quality with kings among queens. The reward for his labour is made special in the ritualistic washing and in his contemplation of the immaculate coins.

NOTES AND GLOSSARY:

grease-proofed: wrapped in paper specially coated to keep oily or fatty foods from leaking

digger: a mechanical plough which lifts the potatoes to the surface

drills: rows in which the potatoes are planted

Irish: each autumn many hundreds of Irish men and women came to Lowland Scotland to earn money by working on farms at harvest time

sideways-bolted: thrown sharply and slyly

enlarging ... magnets of the earth: growing heavier and heavier with the

	heavy, wet soil sticking to them, which made movement difficult
bedraggled:	wet, dirty and untidy
collusions:	conspiracies, improper arrangements
happy rancour:	a mixture of bitterness or resentment and acceptance
howkers:	Scots word for potato gatherers
byre:	Scots word for cowshed
labour:	workforce
pennies:	large copper coloured coins of low value
of the realm:	legal tender, real money
florins:	silver coins worth two shillings or twenty-four pennies
clotted:	coated with mud
English kings:	the royal face (probably George VI) on the silver coins. Scots often see the royal family as English rather than British
Britannias:	the emblem of Great Britain on one side of pennies: Britannia was depicted as a helmeted female warrior carrying a spear

'Lamp-posts'

This is a flight of fancy around an everyday object. Prompted by the sight of some discarded lamp-posts, the poet imaginatively provides them with a past when they witnessed various forms of human behaviour.

COMMENTARY:
Some people take the view that poems are always impassioned, lyrical declarations, and they like to quote Wordsworth who said that '[poetry] takes its origin from emotion recollected in tranquillity'. Many poems in many cultures, however, have less grandiose and inspired origins. One of the oldest kinds of poem is the riddle which asks the reader to decipher an ingenious set of descriptions of a common object. Related to the riddle is the poem which begins like a challenge – 'I bet you cannot write a poem about . . .?' – and the subject offered is deemed unsuitable or uninspiring. In 'Lamp-posts', as in the next poem to be discussed, 'Ratatouille', Dunn takes an unpoetical subject and brings out a poetic quality in it. Lamp-posts are usually assessed for their functional rather than their aesthetic capabilities but he ranges through periods and situations to show them as crucial witnesses to, and even participants in, historic events.

The poem's point of origin is described in the final five lines, and the poem moves towards it or back to it in a series of descriptive strokes. If the reader tries reading through the sequence of situations as if the title was not given the nature of what is described in such varied terms is remarkably mysterious. 'Lamps' and 'lamp-posts' are mentioned only in lines 18 and 22, and even at the end, after the riddle has been solved, Dunn personifies the lamp-posts as weary, defeated people. Perhaps they have observed too much human cruelty and now wish to avert their gaze. Perhaps Dunn is suggesting a causal connection between the luxurious glamour of earlier periods and the atrocities of the twentieth century. The rich vocabulary, foreign phrases, names of authors and cities, all emphasise the continental sweep of the poem. The poet enters the poem personally only in the fifth line from the end, and the 'therefore' connects his feelings to the earlier series of observations as if the conclusion were inevitable.

NOTES AND GLOSSARY:

Ornate ... winged: he is describing the elaborate shapes of old lamp-posts: 'plush' means costly; 'stooped' means curved down; 'fluted' means grooved

boulevardiers: smart, leisurely men-about-town

commissionaires: uniformed doormen at public buildings

savoir faire: sophisticated social skills

Baudelaire: Charles Baudelaire (1821–67), French poet, famous for a lavish, decadent sensibility and associated with Paris

Kafkas: Franz Kafka (1883–1924), German-speaking Czech novelist, noted for his nightmarish vision of the incomprehensibility of life, associated with Prague

Touting: begging, or selling their services

epaulettes: gold braid ornaments worn on the shoulders (he is describing the light falling on the arms of the lamp-posts)

footmen: servants

Habsburgian: belonging to one of the most powerful royal families in Europe from medieval times till 1918, which provided rulers for Spain, Central Europe and the Holy Roman Empire. Vienna became the centre of their power

slipper: dancing shoe (as in the story of Cinderella)

pulse/Of gas-light: momentary brightness under a gas lamp

equerry: an officer attendant upon a member of the royal family

rehabilitated: restored to former good condition (also used of political dissidents who have become acceptable again to a dictatorial government)

Warsaw: the capital of Poland, notorious in the Second World War for some vicious acts of violence and revenge

gallows:	an upright post with cross bar on which people are hanged. (In the French Revolution, during the Terror, 1792–6, the cry of the mob when demanding an aristocrat's death was 'A la lanterne!': 'to the lamp-post!')
municipal:	officially belonging to the town or city

'Ratatouille'

The poem consists of an appreciation of ratatouille, a recipe for the dish, and a connection declared between the dish and other pleasurable and beneficent elements in human life.

COMMENTARY:

Written in loose pentameter lines, as are many of Dunn's poems commented on so far, this one has a markedly different flow from 'Lampposts'. Where the previous poem has six sentences in twenty-six lines, the first and third sections of 'Ratatouille' have thirteen in twenty-two lines; the middle section is different again and has only two sentences in its twenty-two lines. This varying of the shapes of sentences across the poem fits in with the several aspects of the subject matter indicated in the summary above. The opening suggests a demonstration: 'Consider, please', and goes on to enlist support, 'Come ... and unite!' The third section works through imperatives to involve the reader: 'Cook ... serve', 'Eat', 'Believe me', 'Acquire', 'Prepare', 'ask'. In the middle is the making of the ratatouille and the declaration that the pleasure taken in ingredients and cooking is intimately related to certain values and attitudes in men. The elaborateness of the description of the ingredients is indicative of the poet's own enjoyment and generosity. To make and enjoy ratatouille, the poet asserts, is equivalent to making love and abhorring strife: the poem is a recipe for peace.

NOTES AND GLOSSARY:

ratatouille:	a vegetable casserole made as described in the poem and associated particularly with the South of France
invade Afghanistan:	the Soviet Union invaded Afghanistan in 1979
boycott ... Games:	the USA withdrew its team of athletes from the Olympic Games held in Moscow in 1980
Raoul Dufy:	a popular French painter (1877–1953) whose work is characterised by a light, cheerful style and bright colours
playboy:	a rich man who devotes himself to ostentatious pleasures
Salade niçoise:	a salad characteristic of Nice in the South of France.

The ingredients vary but usually include black olives, anchovies, tomatoes, garlic and hard-boiled eggs. It is eaten as a first course

phoney recipes: bogus versions of ratatouille

Leonid Brezhnev: leader of the Soviet Union when poem was published

Ronald Reagan: president of the USA when poem was published

pacific: peaceful

ail: (*French*) garlic

pommes d'amour: (*French*) love apples, that is, tomatoes

bouquet garni: (*French*) a small bunch of herbs, usually tied in muslin

fixtures: sports arrangements

Northern: from northern Europe

Provence: an area in the South of France

Poems from *Elegies* (1985)

Just over half of the poems in this collection are included in *Selected Poems 1964–1983*. The poems were written in the year and a half following the death of Dunn's first wife in 1981 and, apart from memories which go back earlier, cover events dating from the diagnosis of a melanoma, a malignant cancerous growth, behind her eye, to her death and its aftermath. Although the collection was completed before the end of 1982, it was not published until 1985. While writing the poems, Dunn felt beset by doubts and reservations concerning such elegiac writing and, indeed, he still refuses to read the poems in public. When the collection appeared, however, it was warmly received by reviewers, widely appreciated by readers and also won the prestigious Whitbread Prize. To many people dealing with a serious illness or trying to cope with bereavement, the poems speak with unusual directness and have proved uplifting.

It is essential to read the whole sequence because the poems complement, balance and comment on one another; if read in isolation or in a selection, the individual poems may seem sentimental, private, whimsical, detached, morbid or even cynical. They are, nonetheless, public poems, not extracts from a private journal, and Dunn's aim is not for sympathy or tears but to work towards some understanding of his own emotions and, in doing so, engage the interest of readers. He shows in the poems that he is well aware of the ethical and artistic dangers in such an undertaking and insists that there is a base of fact which cannot be fictionalised or, as he puts it, 'Cancer's no metaphor' ('Anniversaries'). It is impossible for a practised poet to write without calculation and without hearing traces of other poets in the linguistic formulations: his personal story is 'Narrated through the legendary, retrospective fictions' ('The Stories'). In the same poem, Dunn concedes that 'Grief has its own

romance, its comedy,/Its preposterous and selfish gestures', and he in-
dulges in a fantasy of how he could or could not escape from his grief in.
the sort of heroic exploits associated with nineteenth century figures such
as General Gordon, who was stabbed to death in Khartoum in 1885, and
the missionary explorer David Livingstone, who died in central Africa in
1873. A tendency to see and express experiences in a literary manner is
evident in the references to models and precedents, for example, Pascal
and Shakespeare, but in 'Tursac' he hears his wife's rebuke: ' "Write out
of me, not out of what you read" '. In many of the poems there is a
concern with matters of aesthetic taste, sometimes beautiful objects, sometimes sensitive discriminations. This taste is not something imposed on
experiences or something unique to Douglas Dunn. It is a demonstration of
the artistic sensibility of his wife and a tribute to how much he learned
from her: 'She taught me how to live, then how to die,/And I curate
her dreams and gallery' ('Writing with Light'). Their house (called 'The
Butterfly House') was the centre of their shared taste and is celebrated in a
number of poems. In the *Selected Poems*, Dunn excludes many of these
poems perhaps because their points are established by other poems and
because, out of the context of the whole collection, they may seem too
private; 'The Butterfly House', 'Writing with Light', 'Attics' and 'Dining'
are examples. An aspect of their shared taste was an affection for France.
In 1972 they had lived for several months at Tursac in south-west France
and enjoyed the locality, the food and the style of life. The use of French
words, for example in 'France' and 'Creatures', attempts to give the feel,
the foreignness and the intimacy, of France.

Several procedures can be discerned in the arrangement of the poems
in *Elegies*. A temporal progression moves from the early stages of the
couple's romance in 1962 to his discovery of a new partner in 1982.
The selection of events during this stretch of twenty years is extremely
partial and centres very obviously on instances and emotions related to
Lesley's death. The book is neither a biography, nor an autobiography, nor
even a documentary on a marriage. The opening poem (not included in
Selected Poems) is called 'Re-reading Katherine Mansfield's *Bliss and
Other Stories*' and introduces several motifs of the collection. Dunn dis-
covers the 'skeleton of gauze' of a fly trapped almost twenty years earlier
when he had been reading the story entitled 'Bliss'. The arbitrariness of
the frail creature's sudden death when in a state of bliss contains a touching irony for the poet: back in 1962 when he was reading the story he was
falling in love and the situation was full of promise. The poem does not
push a crude parallel at the reader, but the sad outcome is there in the
final lines: 'and this, this fly, verbosely buried/In "Bliss", one dry tear
punctuating "Bliss" '. The word 'verbosely', meaning with ponderous
words, for the creature trapped in a book, indicates Dunn's worry that in
Elegies he may turn his dead wife into a poetic exhibit.

The second poem, 'The Butterfly House' (not included in *Selected Poems*), introduces their home in Hull, the house of their life together and of her dying. The third poem, 'Second Opinion', spells out much more directly what has taken place: the descent into misery is irrevocable. The whole collection divides in the middle. In all, there are thirty-nine poems. The first twenty, up to and including 'Creatures', concentrate mainly on what has happened up to the time of writing; the remaining nineteen, while often looking back, are less retrospective and more focused on Dunn's struggle to cope with his bereavement. Across the complete sequence he varies the stimulus to the reader. There is a wide variety of verse forms, including different sorts of sonnet, terza rima, blank verse, rhyming quatrains and quintets, and free verse. Longer poems alternate with shorter ones and some are more cheerful, some gloomier; some more physical, some spiritual; some more private, some more detached. The imagery is drawn from many sources although a tendency emerges to see emotional changes in terms of the changing seasons. Weather, trees, the sky, birds, the sea, fruits – all act as correlatives to his moods and many of his memories relate to scenes and times of the year. Ideas of melting recur: melting into tears, a loss of firmness, past and present running together, one condition sliding into another, the physical becoming ghostly. In the title 'Transblucency' (not in *Selected Poems*) he runs together Blues music, different blues of sky and sea, translucence and an interplay between states of mind and himself and his wife. The poem concludes:

> The lights of Newport rinse in the tide,
> Then one by one disperse, as life dissolves
> Into the deity within ourselves

More so than in any of his previous collections, Dunn faces his own emotional self and probes the qualities he respects and on which he can rely. In the situation of death, loss and solitude, he has to concede that his strength is very limited. Poetry itself, the struggle with language and form, helps as a therapy and often the gloom is contained by the delicacy and vividness of the poetry. Some critics might object that his dead wife, Lesley, emerges as flawless. Did she have no faults? Did they have no rows? The sequence, however, is a commemoration of her and, more particularly, of her extraordinary, cheerful stoicism in the face of pain and dying, and an exploration of Dunn's own sense of desolation. Humour is present at times. In many of the poems a spiritual quality is strong and sometimes his wife is invested with saintly or religious attributes (see the conclusions of 'Creatures' and 'Reincarnations'). In Western culture it is difficult to write of the spiritual without using terms which have been developed or appropriated by the Christian religion. In fact, nothing theological or doctrinal is advanced and what impresses many readers is the profoundly human anguish, endurance, love and blessing.

The epigraph from Giosuè Carducci (Italian poet, 1835–1907; Nobel Prize 1906) can be translated as follows:

Be of good cheer, O weary humans!
Everything passes on and nothing can die.
We have hated and suffered too much. But love!
The world is beautiful and the future is blessed.

In the Notes I have tried to offer information and help with a representative selection of the poems (see also the Sample Answer for comments on 'Birch Room' and 'The Clear Day'). In all, I have dealt with more than one third of the poems in *Elegies*.

'Second Opinion'

This is the third poem in the whole sequence. It describes the visit to a medical specialist in Leeds who diagnoses that Dunn's wife has a malignant melanoma behind her eye. The main focus is on Dunn's reactions to the situation in the waiting-room and to the diagnosis.

COMMENTARY:
The feel of this poem is constrained and jerky. There is nothing lavish in imagery, rhythm or syntax. The short sentences in lines 1, 8, 9, 11, 12, 14 and 18 keep arresting any flow; the questions in lines 9–10, 11, 12, and 14 have a similar effect. Although the poem is written in four-line stanzas there is no consistency of length of line, no obvious metre and no rhyme. Another factor which contributes to a disjointedness is the absence of the wife. After she arrives with him in line 1 she becomes separate and is referred to as 'she'. It is as if the diagnosis of the illness created an immediate gap which cannot be crossed: 'My body ached to suffer like her twin/And touch the cure with lips and healing sesames'. In the penultimate stanza the blankness of the gap is presented in a series of absences: no image on which to focus, no last straw even to which he could cling, no comforting aspect of familiar nature, nothing on which the senses can fasten. The mind, too, is out of its depth and cannot grasp events or contemplate something huge such as 'destiny'. The doctor tries his best to be informative and sympathetic but is reduced to a series of practised gestures, conveyed in 'professional' and 'medical'. He seems so young and inexperienced, and even his wedding ring emphasises a difference from, rather than a similarity to Dunn, soon to lose his wife.

On a re-reading of the poem, the 'apparently well' in line 3 functions as a dramatic irony and, with the 'bandaged eyes', 'dark spectacles' and 'a pad over one eye', anticipates the horrible revelation about to be made. The further cruel irony of his wife, an artist, being diseased in her eye, the first instrument of her art, seems inevitable and spiteful ('malignancy').

NOTES AND GLOSSARY:

Leeds:	a large city in Yorkshire
second opinion:	consultation with a second doctor to check on an earlier diagnosis
warned:	told to keep still (while their mother is examined by the doctor)
Malignancy:	tendency to cause harm; invasive cancer which may resist medical treatment
there:	her eye. (We know this from details in other poems in *Elegies*)
twin:	twins often have a strange sympathy with each other's pains and pleasures even at a distance
touch . . . lips:	like a parent kissing a child better when it suffers a minor injury
sesames:	magic spells

'Thirteen Steps and the Thirteenth of March'

The date is the day of his wife's death in 1981, and the steps are the stairs leading from the pantry to the bedroom in his house. He juxtaposes visits by friends, a public aspect, and his seclusion with her, their privacy, in the final stages of her illness.

COMMENTARY:

The title with its 'thirteen' and 'thirteenth' announces a double un-luckiness and a further unlucky thirteen is found in lines 11–12. Although sadness and dying are at the heart of the poem, there is a decided balance of pleasures with the pain: the very inevitability of death concentrates the minds of those involved, and the whole composition is a celebration as much as a lament. The stoicism of the dying woman, her resolute good spirits (lines 6 and 24) and her 'understated mischief' (line 18), have a calming effect on her visitors. The second half is more intimate, with the focus more on the relationship between Dunn and his wife. Despite the terminal nature of her illness, they could sometimes suspend time so that their past became present (line 28), each moment was 'unique' (line 37), and the future was held at bay (lines 42–3). They could forget themselves and their situation 'in words and music' and find release in games. The poem does not have a progression or chronological narrative except that the final stanza is set after her death, and the rest of the poem is set in the period before her death. The actual dying does not feature. The working of the poem is cumulative, and the mixture of domestic social chores is intertwined with the private griefs and pleasures. In form, the poem looks quite regular, with its stanzas of four lines usually with five stresses, but the movement of the poetry is not so smooth. In only one case does a sentence run for the whole stanza; in all others small sentences are stitched together or set alongside each other as a series of events and impressions. The shifting manner of the recollection strikes us as more realistic, and the switch from duties to emotions and from the visitors to the married couple helps to guard against self-pity and sentimentality. There is even quiet, self-deprecating humour in evidence.

NOTES AND GLOSSARY:

butler: the servant in a house who answers the door and attends to the needs of the hosts and their guests

pantry: a small cold store-room, often situated next to the kitchen, where such things as drinks, glasses and food are kept

cyclamen: a winter-flowering pot plant

trusty tributes: reliable attention

holding . . . real: counteracting the unpleasantness of the situation (of illness and imminent death)

the grief: her actual death

Turning . . . lucidity: choosing to remain clear-headed rather than take drugs to blur her sensation of pain

candlelight: softer on the patient's sight (and possibly for romantic reasons)

John . . . the last: Lesley Dunn was curator at an art gallery, and her advice continued to be sought by artists planning their exhibitions

Bequests: personal possessions to be given to people after her death

conspiracy: agreement (not hostile but possibly secret)

candle-shadows . . . fingers: making shadow shapes on the wall with their hands

Time: personified to resemble a landlord or boss who leaves the house to take the dog for a walk round the suburban streets with their garden walls and hedges of privet

Her fingers dwindled: she lost weight as the cancer advanced and so her wedding ring no longer fitted

the Newland Park: a hotel near where her funeral takes place

ironic . . . loyalty: he finds it strange, incongruous, like a false echo, that the ritual of tea and sherry being served should take place again (after his wife's death); and he feels, in a mild way, that he is forcing the mourners to repeat the process just because they were friends and had visited his wife before she died when he had to serve them drinks from his pantry

'Arrangements'

After a death, certain official procedures require to be completed. The facts of the death must be registered at the Regstrar's office. The Registrar is also responsible for registering births and marriages and, in secular cases, the Registrar performs the wedding ceremony. The poem describes the occasion when, Dunn, accompanied by his father-in-law, went to register the death of his wife.

COMMENTARY:

When you have read the poem and had a chance to reflect on it, you will notice that the title contains several ambiguities. 'Arrangements' is the bland or euphemistic word used to describe the official and often distressing procedures necessary after a death. We also employ the word to describe plans made for the future but the poem proposes no substantial future for the author. The word suggests tidiness and order but the poem reveals confusion. The very first line announces uncertainties: ' "Is this the door?" This must be it. No, no.'

A central image in the poem is of doors, of entering and leaving. The Registrar's office keeps a record of the crossing of what are publicly seen as major thresholds: birth, marriage and death. In the opening secion, the door leads to the wedding celebrations, symbolic of hope. By the fifth and final section, the poet finds himself at a different door, the door of the undertaker. The whole process of life, of beginnings and endings, flows through the office, and in the poem the stages, which are usually considered as separate, are curiously mingled. In the second section, the poet and the newly widowed woman are said to share a birthday (line 29) and they seem to be tied together as if in a form of marriage ('bond', 'Good wishes', 'friends for ever'). Also, he is aware that with his gloom he can, if he intrudes on a wedding ceremony, contaminate what should be a happy event: 'They must not see me. I bear a tell-tale scar.' Earlier (line 10), he looks back to his own wedding and is aware that a similar intrusion must have taken place: 'Death, too, must have looked in on our wedding.' Such parallels, overlaps, comparisons and contrasts run through the whole poem, just as the confetti of celebration sticks to the mourning widow (line 21).

The other main clash or discrepancy in the poem is between the routine bureaucracy of the Registrar's office and the extremities of emotion, happiness and grief, of the clients. The 'municipal function', the 'tabulations', cannot accommodate the 'whimsical bridesmaids', the 'terrible bond' between the bereaved and the 'comfortless words, "waste", "untimely", "tragic" '. The ordinariness of the language and the unrhymed verse allow the drab glumness of Dunn to communicate itself to the reader. The bereaved poet feels himself 'digested in statistics of love' and the reader comes to understand something of the particularity and the anonymity of someone else's grief.

NOTES AND GLOSSARY:

whimsical: fanciful, full of thoughts of future happiness

municipal function: the dull routine of official procedures

'heart attack': on the official form, the doctor has written a technical term for heart attack and the woman does not understand the term

Already gossiped ... conversations: the phrases used by people discussing the death and offering sympathy to the bereaved ('obit.' is an abbreviation for obituary, marking a death)

On the promenades ... "sympathy" and dinners (lines 27–34): Dunn is imagining the kinds of therapeutic holidays undertaken by bereaved people in order to escape or recover from their grief

promenades: walks on the seafront at coastal resorts

insurance: life insurance, paid by an insurance company to the beneficiary on the death of a person

sanatoria: establishments where one can recover from illness

predestinations: fixed prospects for the future

Fictitious clinics: private hospitals either as imagined and presented in novels or making false claims as to their usefulness

Prefab'd: (short for prefabricated) built of ready-made sections assembled on the site

bijou: pretty in a clichéd style

antiseptic Alps: Swiss mountains, high and clear-aired, famous for sanatoria

distilled ... drink: purified but, in this case, the process by which alcohol in spirits is refined (Dunn recounts elsewhere that he drank heavily after his wife's death)

hideaway: unflamboyant, furtive

tabulations: arrangements of facts

morbid: gloomy, concerned with death

genealogy: the sequence of ancestors and descendants in a family

cipher: insignificant figure, one of many

recording angel: semi-biblical figure supposed to register each good and bad act of every human being

-oma: (*Greek*) word for tumour (Dunn's wife died of a melanoma)

taboo: deliberately inconspicuous (becasue death is a forbidden subject)

tell-tale scar: the mark of death and mourning

digested . . . love:	submerged in the details of marriages
Sub-gothic:	imitation of elaborate medieval church design
leaded windows:	with small panes of glass set in lead frames
We:	he and his wife

France

France and personal memories of shared visits to it recur in a number of the poems in *Elegies*. This is one of half a dozen sonnets in the sequence.

COMMENTARY:
Time, love and death have been subjects in sonnets since the sixteenth century and are prominent motifs in Shakespeare's sonnet sequence written in the 1590s. The tightness of the form and its very brevity force the poet to be concise, and the dramatic situation is presented in a very condensed way which expands in the mind of the reader. Larger horizons of the past and of a suggested future prompt our imaginations. Some of the rhymes make very suggestive combinations: 'frost' . . . 'ghost', 'passers-by' . . . 'when I die', 'gone away' . . . 'Some other day', and the word *'jouissance'* persuades us to pronounce 'France' in the French manner. The syntax, too, operates very compactly in the confines of the lines and rhymes of the sonnet. Dialogue is accommodated very dexterously and pronouns are manipulated with nimbleness. The whole ordering of the poem is beautifully judged. For example, line 7 seems to interrupt the flow as if it were stuck in the wrong place; but the jump from the present into the future between the passers-by looking up and the flowers on the window sill catches the mind of the wife and her apprehensions. The winter frost (line 1) confronts the recalled summers in France; the flowers brought by well-wishers are like but unlike the meadows of line 12; the sparrows play, while the husband and wife cannot; the pale ghost-like figures at the window anticipate the final line and 'Some other day'.

NOTES AND GLOSSARY:

scuttled:	moved quickly but awkwardly
ghost . . . duplicate:	the poet's wife in her pale nightgown is dying, and he feels that he shares her condition
draw the curtains:	curtains were traditionally drawn at the windows of the room where someone died
***jouissance*:**	(*French*) enjoyment, (sexual) pleasure

'Sandra's Mobile'

The poem celebrates Dunn's wife as an artist and describes how a piece of art acted as an emblem of their love on the night of her death. Another poem in *Elegies* centred on a mobile is 'A Silver Air Force' (not included in *Selected Poems 1964–1983*).

COMMENTARY:
Turning as it does on value words such as 'constant', 'loyal', 'comradeship', 'love' and 'prove' the poem operates like a mobile. The concluding couplet, holding together in rhyme 'love' and 'dove', offers the transformation, as each of the three gulls spins, of the ordinary into the extraordinary and of the individual into a unity. The Shakespearean sonnet with its three quatrains is pulled to a conclusion in the neat couplet. The sentence in line 9, ' "Blow on them, Love" ', can be read most obviously as a request by his wife to the poet to stir the mobile with his breath but it can also suggest the possibility, particularly with its capital L, that Love is being involved to provide its animating breath, and later it is love which is 'crowned' and given the glory.

NOTES AND GLOSSARY:

Sandra:	a close friend
mobile:	a construction with balanced parts which, when suspended in mid-air, moves in the draughts of air
disinterested:	impartial (her loyalty is to artistic rightness)
indoor sky:	the ceiling
thermals:	currents of rising air caused by inequalities of temperature in different parts of a landscape
dove:	a bird associated with peace; also, as a turtle dove, with love; also, in the New Testament, with the Holy Spirit or Comforter who helps Christians in the absence of Christ

'Empty Wardrobes'

A painful part of the aftermath of a death involves the next-of-kin sorting out the belongings of the deceased and disposing of many of them. This necessity causes Dunn to think back to shopping with his wife for dresses.

COMMENTARY:
The first line of stanza two is crucial to our understanding of the poem: 'Clothes are a way of exercising love' can be read in several ways which open up aspects of the whole poem. First, clothes can be chosen and worn to show love for another person. Or clothes can be made or bought as a gift, a token of love. Dressing up and experimenting with different clothes can be a means of training or extending notions of love. We learn in this poem and others that Dunn's wife had been fond of clothes and that he had often accompanied her on shopping expeditions. He took pleasure in the

routine of her trying on dresses and showing herself off for his evaluation. He remembers different events: happy moments when a dress held them together and less happy ones such as he describes in the second last stanza. The fourth stanza contains three different times: when she chose the green dress (the conclusion to what is described in the previous stanza); when she rediscovered the dress as she was going through her clothes just before her death; and his smelling of the pot-pourri in the present which also prompts various other memories. She had decided, in advance of her death, which of her clothes she would offer as gifts to her friends and, in their wearing of her clothes, they carry something of her into the future.

The mood of the poem is not monotonous: sliding from the mild self-mockery of the opening stanza; to a more lavish, 'romantic' middle section; lapsing into regret in stanza five; and concluding in an emptiness of grief. The final emptiness is anticipated in the title with its suggestion of the absence of what had given colour and warmth to life. Although the rhyme scheme is intricate and regular, the poem reads not as mechanical or jaunty but as rather subdued and private. Throughout, there is an element of doubt as if Dunn was aware of having played only a supporting role (see opening stanza), was not fully confident of his own statemnt in stanza two, distrusted his ability to enter into the game (stanza five), and, without his leading lady, the play collapses and he is left bereft.

NOTES AND GLOSSARY:

dapper: neat in appearance and smartly dressed

young ambassador ... star: role models for Dunn of well-groomed, sophisticated men of the world

rake: nonchalant, dissolute man of fashion

Rachmaninov: Serge Rachmaninov (1873–1943), Russion composer and pianist, famous for his lushly romantic style of music

ploy: game, adventure

flounced: showed herself off dramatically

cabin trunk: deep chest such as was used on board ships in earlier times

pot-pourri: mixture of dried flower petals employed to give off a mild fragrance

full of where and when: the fragrance reminded him powerfully of places and times

memorial key: the pot-pourri evokes (is a memorial to) his wife; many memories are triggered by the scent

franc-less: lacking money (French francs)

husbandly: with the authority of a husband; 'to husband' also means to save or guard resources

hangers: racks of clothes

Lafayette:	name of famous department store in Paris
couturier:	person who designs, makes and sells fashionable clothes (French word)
needlewoman:	woman who makes or sews together dresses. (The images of sewing possibly allude to the Greek myth of the Fates who spin the thread of individual lives and decide when to cut it in death)
finery:	expensive decorations and clothes
keepsakes:	gifts which remind the receiver of the giver

'A Summer Night'

More than a year has passed since Dunn's wife died, and the poem takes stock of where he has reached in coping with his loss.

COMMENTARY:

About one third of all the poems in *Elegies* begin with a single-sentence opening line. It may set the scene, make a declaration or introduce a central image. In this poem we may, after we have read through the poem, see the opening line as performing all three of these functions. In fact, most of the sentences are short and, in the lines of blank verse of the same length, they read as a series of mental adjustments, and the only sense of an expansionist mood comes in the penultimate sentence, the longest in the poem, and in the defiance of the final two lines.

Nightfall, when the business and sociability of the day are past and the emptiness of the dark night lies ahead, is often the most difficult time for bereaved and lonely people. The evening has its own beauty (lines 1–3) but for Dunn there is no peace; rather, his nights are troubled by delusions and fantasies which he struggles to ignore. He tries to identify with the two birch trees in the garden which he and his wife had planted as tokens of their love but the trees remain trees and 'have their own two lives to lead'. Nonetheless, in the concluding portion of the poem, he returns to the trees as symbols of young love and finds some solace in 'a cool silence/Composed of green'. Before he has succeeded with that manoeuvre, he describes how, during the year since his wife's death, he has bumped from day to day, season to season and there has seemed to be no progress, only a repetition of pain. The borrowed 'fortitude' he takes from his cherished memories and the emblematic twin trees anchors temporarily his 'floating life' and allows him to assert the perpetuation of their love: 'A small white cry, one last wild, stubborn rose'.

NOTES AND GLOSSARY:

Rhythmical ... cadences: the two phrases are very similar and describe the coming and going or wafting of scents from the garden

bedroom of the world: he generalises his own situation

This telephone ... credit: he imagines innumerable farewell messages from his dead wife, and she has no bill to pay

aromatic: scented (birch trees have a very distinctive smell in early summer)

pulchritudes: physical beauties, essences

four degrees ... shades: the different temperatures and shadows of the four seasons

Francis: Saint Francis of Assisi (1182–1226), a man of simple piety who blessed the birds and felt blessed by them

fortitude: strength of mind, resolution

white: pure, clean, bright in contrast to the darkness (see following note)

one ... rose: sometimes a single rose on a bush survives when all the others have gone; wild roses are small and sometimes white

---

'Reading Pascal in the Lowlands'

This is one of the very few poems in *Elegies* where Dunn emerges, at least in part, from the privacy of his own sorrow to see another's grief. One concern of the poem is precisely how engrossed individuals become in their own situation and, therefore, how they fail to notice someone else's predicament.

COMMENTARY:

Several perspectives came into operation in the poem: the poet-narrator has his private sorrow (which we know about because the poem is part of a sequence), undisclosed to anyone else in the park; the tragedy of the family with their young son dying of leukaemia emerges; a summer's evening in the park offers its pleasures; and at the end the poet looks down from a hill at the town with its (apparently) 'undramatic streets'. A gradual narrative develops through the six 7-line stanzas. There is no rhyme scheme but some rhymes and approximations to rhyme occur, giving a reminder of ordering but no predictable pattern to the lines. Each line has four or five stresses but no metrical regularity forces the pace of the meandering narrative.

The title indicates something incongruous: the seventeenth-century French scientific thinker does not immediately seem appropriate to a small town in Lowland Scotland. Echoes are stirred of other titles of poems such as 'Wordsworth in the Tropics' (Aldous Huxley) and 'Ovid in the Third Reich' (Geoffrey Hill) where a similar incongruity is explored. In Dunn's poem the point of Pascal becomes apparent only in the fourth and fifth stanzas. For the bereaved poet, reading Pascal has been a rewarding experience (lines 23–4), but the very fact that he is reading a book and, particularly, a serious book by a foreign author of centuries before, brands him as alien and unsympathetic in the eyes of the gloomy father. The father is so absorbed in his family unhappiness that he cannot imagine the stranger on the bench can possibly understand the situation much less be coping with his own grievous loss. Dunn realises (stanza 4) that the man's misery will not be alleviated by hearing of 'my own sorrows': each unhappiness seems unique. Although 'concern' is announced in the opening line, and the wheelchair indicates something wrong, the actual problem emerges only gradually and is confirmed in the single directly spoken word in the poem, 'Leukaemia'. The whole procedure is very indirect but hints of an unsatisfactory mood are given in the description of the shadows as 'Bickering and falling', the separate movements of the members of the family, the man's tentative smile which 'falls at my feet', and the 'shuffled over and ungrassed' area in front on the bench. The apparent randomness of the noise of a swing, runners jogging by at a distance, the fishing, the sunlight accentuates the isolation of the sadness.

NOTES AND GLOSSARY:

Pascal:	Blaise Pascal (1623–62), French scientist and thinker. Two books by him were published, one, *Les Pensées*, after his death
Lowlands:	an area in Scotland south and east of the Highlands
Bickering:	coming and going, contending with each other
picks tobacco:	in order to make a (roll-up) cigarette
Leukaemia:	cancer of the blood cells
***Pensées*:**	Pascal's collection of *Thoughts* (1670) on such subjects as religion, reason and feeling. He saw life as deeply paradoxical
light with meditation:	light-headed or detached as a result of thinking (rather than action)
religiose:	enclosed and self-aware in a religious state of mind
mystic . . . solitude:	abstracted after a day spent on his own
premonition:	warning or fear concerning the future
perimeter:	outer limits (of the park)
bracken:	a kind of fern
gorse:	thorn bush, whin
panoptic:	with a complete or panoramic view

'Land Love'

The poet recollects an occasion with his wife sometime before her death and he continues the recollection into the present, imagining that she is still with him.

COMMENTARY:
The terza rima form parallels the pattern of thought central to this poem. The second line of each tercet (three-line unit) provides the rhyme sound of the first and third lines of the following tercet so that there is a constant linkage of present to future and also present to past. The rhymes, however, are usually unobvious, partly because they are often inexact, partly because each stanza ends with a full stop which enforces a gap before the rhyme is completed. Two changes take place in the third stanza: the tense shifts from past to present, and the 'we' of the first two stanzas disappears. Most of the memories or imaginings are set in the dusk but night comes on in the final stanza. Dunn creates a sense of immediacy and intensity by using clipped sentences of statement and a metaphorical compression, for example, 'Dusk was an insect-hovered dark water' and 'Night is its Dog Star'. Also, although the poem deals mainly with recollections, an air of expectancy is conveyed in the acute awareness of small movements and in phrases such as 'Dusk is a listening', 'She waits at the door' and the question, 'What rustles in the leaves . . .?' In the dusk, between the day and the night, a time of reverie, there is an openness to the spiritual or ethereal, even a slight undercurrent of religious, biblical suggestion: 'saints', 'grace', 'starry sheaves', 'fields of life' or, as he puts it more directly, 'a half-heard religious anecdote'. In the penultimate stanza he introduces the image of the still, floating swans as emblematic of the 'private grace of man and wife'. The 'white poise' of swans and lovers glances back to the 'coupledom of us' in the opening line. The whole poem keeps moving between an alertness to the moment and place and a mysterious negation of time and space to demonstrate that love transcends the usual compartmentalising and is manifest 'in the remote/Local August that is everywhere and here'. His dead wife has come to be identified with aspects of nature and, accordingly, to live on in them and transform them.

NOTES AND GLOSSARY:
coupledom: being together as a pair
saints . . . nimbus: as the trout leap out of the water they create rings on the surface which look like haloes, the representation in art of the light which was reputed to surround the heads of saintly people
night-boys: boys playing in the dark
at the door of the hemisphere: he imagines her at the threshold (between summer and autumn, day and night, the human and the natural, living and dead)
half-heard . . . anecdote: he seems to wish for a sign from his dead wife, some sort of religious revelation
monogamous: swans are reputed to remain loyal to their mates as long as they live

Picture:	reflect (in the calm water) and act as an image of
Dog star:	Sirius, the brightest star
eyelet:	small hole, peep-hole
sheaves:	bundles of corn, constellations

'Home Again'

Returning home after an absence of six weeks, the poet is overwhelmed by his sensory impressions of the place. The poem charts his observations, and reactions to them.

COMMENTARY:

This is a particularly obvious example of how a reader's knowledge of the death of the poet's wife and the sequence, *Elegies*, affects a reading of the poem. There is no clear reference to his dead wife until half a dozen lines from the end and, up to that point, a reader considering the poem in isolation could see it as a rather extravagant piece possibly intended to be humorous. Dunn appears to take a grim relish in going through the inventory of the contents of his house. When we do know the context of the poem we understand that the described items act as analogies for his emotions of loss, loneliness, nostalgia, separation and even guilt. Images of neglect, decay and death predominate in the first sixteen lines, for example, in 'Cadaver', 'orphanage', 'rust', 'withered', 'mortuary', 'emaciations', 'absence'. Everything in the house which had been fresh and edible has, as it were, participated in the death of his wife, and he is left as the sole living thing: 'It is very lonely on the green settee'. There is a brief respite in an escapist fantasy (Lines 20–5) but the empti-ness of the house reasserts its hold on him, and the finality of death seems absolute. Nonetheless, against the pressure of such negativity a positive surge takes place, and the poem concludes on a note of exultation. The flowers in the vase have shed their petals and, in imagining their fall, he is taken back to the full beauty they displayed and he experiences, like them, a 'botanic ecstasy'. His dead wife is restored to him spiritually in his vision of the flowers, and the chilling emptiness is rebuffed when he calls her name and finds it 'very strange and wonderful'. The title of the poem, 'Home Again', which had seemed so mocking and ironic for most of the poem, at the end is straightforwardly, albeit mysteriously, true. Such a revelation emerges miraculously, 'with angelophanous/Secrets', from the listing of items so loaded with his misery; there is no sudden shift in the unobtrusive movement of the verse or the syntax.

NOTES AND GLOSSARY:

aromatics:	fragrant or spicy smells
Chastise:	rebuke, punish

Cadaver:	corpse
orphanage:	a home for parentless children (suggesting that the fruit has been neglected)
Burgundy:	a wine-producing region of France
mortuary:	a building where dead bodies are stored before burial or cremation (a metaphor for the drying up of the life-juice of the grapes)
emaciations:	shrunken shapes
vegetable absence:	nothing is growing. (There may be an echo here of Andrew Marvell's 'vegetable love' in 'To His Coy Mistress')
green:	mouldy
bacterial:	rotten
their foliage ... park:	the patterned green curtains are the only approximations to something growing
there:	in green exotic places (imagined when touching the curtains)
Martagon:	purplish kind of lily
Summerland:	land of perpetual summer
pipes shudder:	the pipes vibrate as the central heating warms up
gnosis:	awareness of spiritual truths
The moon's oasis:	as if the dry-looking moon (time) used the empty house as a source of moisture
aghast:	open in horror
deranged expiry:	disordered or maddened death
zig-zags:	the movement of petals fluttering down
appled:	smelling of apples
Bleaches:	whitens, cleans
angelophanous:	making angels visible to humans

'Anniversaries'

Dates in the year which were special in his relationship with his wife – their first meeting, their wedding, her death, for example – cause a mixture of emotions when they come round now that she is gone. The poem explores some of these emotions.

COMMENTARY:
The poem consists of four sections, each of seventeen lines. In each section four quatrains rhyme ABBA. The opening line of the quatrains has three main stresses, the remaining three lines have four stresses. The seventeenth line, as is indicated by the indentation, follows the three-stress pattern but, in the first three sections, follows the rhyme of lines 14 and 15; the final line of the poem does not rhyme with any other line.

In the original collection, *Elegies*, each section is printed on a separate page with the result that the whole looks more like a sequence than a single poem. Nonetheless, the four sections are intermeshed in various ways and there is a narrative development from the onset of love through the marriage and their life together to her death and his subsequent mourning. The intricacy of the verse form is matched by recurrences and echoes of words and images. For example, the word 'day' appears twelve times and the sky which features in the first three sections receives a new twist in the 'one bright star' at the conclusion of the poem. Throughout, there are shifts from a vast scale of time and space to the particularity of individual moments and locations, from souls to physical details, and from external public events to internal, private thoughts. In many of the elements described in this paragraph, the poem is reminiscent of Shakespeare's *Sonnets*, and the Metaphysical poetry of the seventeenth century. The title itself recalls John Donne's 'Anniversaries' (1611–12) and many phrases manifest an unexpected collocation similar to that found in Metaphysical poets: 'interior clay'; 'wife now to the weather'; 'A vegetable sentiment'; 'starlings in my soul'; 'oceans cradle little seas/That water in the eye'; 'vitreous space'.

Dunn writes with a strong awareness of a tradition of anniversary poems and an awareness also that his individual grief is a repetition of an utterly common experience. His use of literary allusions draws attention to this but does not usually demand from the reader an exact identification of the original; an exception occurs in lines 27–9 (see Notes below). The Latin derivation of 'anniversary' means the turning of the year and the language and verse of the poem emphasise, over and over, notions of recurrence. Death does not draw a final line at the end of a life or delete what has happened: actions and emotions imprint themselves on the continuing cycle and are revived in the memories of surviving people. For the bereaved Dunn, anniversaries of special occasions with his wife bring home to him a desperate sense of loss and helplessness which makes the remembered moments of pleasure painful and unbearably poignant. The first three sections are addressed to his dead wife ('you') but in the fourth he is on his own and 'us' (line 53) is general and includes the reader. The final section is the one where, marking the anniversary of her death, he has most difficulty in finding any consolation or pleasing memory. Nonetheless, the final image, ambivalent as it is, does contain a 'compassionate' element and the unique lack of rhyme gives the final line a special status.

The opening quatrain declares the retentive firmness of the memory and how the past acts on the present. The day when Dunn and his wife-to-be first walked out together is recalled and the pastoral flavour is to be maintained through the peom. Death cannot obliterate the delight experienced on that day but the day's anniversary, in her absence, renders him helpless. (Although his wife was cremated, Dunn presents the dead, her and himself, buried in a tomb and uses a traditional literary vocabulary reminiscent of the seventeenth century). The second section appears to offer a contrast: urban starlings and a fruit market but a consistency proves stronger than the contrasts. The very fruit and vegetables suggest or act as an 'indigenous metaphor' for exotic Shakespearean settings but there is a nightmarish element for him. In his bleak loneliness on the anniversary of their wedding day, he drinks himself into forgetfulness.

The third section differs from the others in that it is concerned not with a specific anniversary but with memories of times of shared pleasure. Images of moisture convey a feeling of melting and mingling, 'when souls rinse/Together in their moist reunions'. Again, Dunn explores his memories and emotions in a context of the natural world: dew, blossoms, birds, oceans and May – the month, according to tradition, of blossoming and love. The promise offered by May has ended in tears and in the fourth section the mood darkens with the anniversary of his wife's death. The main images here are of ungiving opaqueness, of 'thwarted life and snapped increase'. The endeavour of poetry seems futile but, at the very end, the 'bright rain-glass' on the birch tree outside the window is concentrated into 'one bright star,/Cold and compassionate'. The paradox in the last line perhaps contains the remoteness of death and the abiding presence of love.

NOTES AND GLOSSARY:

nomadic:	always moving on
utmost ground:	solid bottom (sailors use the phrase 'holding ground' for a reliable anchorage; theologians use 'ground' to mean the base or foundation of being)
interior clay:	description of the way in which the poet almost unwittingly remains attached to anniversaries
Roukenglen and Kelvingrove:	public parks in Glasgow
Inchinnan:	Dunn's home town, south-west of Glasgow
Rings radiate:	wedding rings light up
bangles:	bracelets left where the bones have decayed away (compare John Donne's poem 'The Relic')
Longanimous:	patient (Latin derivation means 'long-souled')
athletic:	vigorous
Ornithological hurrahs:	exultations of birds
Candleriggs:	street in Glasgow, site of fruit and vegetable market
citric:	such as orange and lemon
vegetable sentiment:	the remains and smells of the produce recall feelings
Indigenous metaphor:	local version of
Arcadian:	idealised rural setting in Greek and Renaissance literature
Bohemian sea-coast ... bear:	reference to Shakespeare's *The Winter's*

Tale (1611). The play is concerned with obsession, loss and renewal. The action spans many years and moves between Sicily and Bohemia. A famous stage direction in Act III reads: 'Exit, pursued by a bear'. There is a horribly surreal quality to parts of the play

null: empty

arboreal aplomb: gusto or self-confidence of trees (in blossom)

day's door hangs ajar: time is suspended and opportunity seems unlimited

souls rinse: as if their spirits wash together

Iambic, feathery Anon: the anonymous birds singing their dawn chorus

oceans . . . eye: the grand scale of Earth carries the tears of individuals

glassy ground: smooth, featureless surface

vitreous space: glassy emptiness

snapped increase: process of fruition cut off

Cancer's no metaphor: disease takes its name metaphorically from the Latin word for crab and 'cancer' is itself often used metaphorically. Dunn is employing our knowledge of the word to insist that, in this instance, cancer is a brutal fact and cannot be softened or translated into metaphor

window's birch: birch tree outside their window (see the poem 'Birch Room')

supernatural: beyond anything he expected to find or could explain

come dusk: as darkness came on

'Leaving Dundee'

The final poem in *Elegies*, this marks very definitely an end of a traumatic part of his life. It also registers certain continuities, overlaps and new beginnings. In the year after his wife's death, Dunn worked as Writer in Residence at the University of Dundee in the east of Scotland.

COMMENTARY:

There is a restless quality in the poem, an in-betweenness, intimated in the title. A bifocal view of Dunn's situation takes different angles: now–then, here–there, up–down, home–away. In the first two lines some change is announced with the opening of a window in the cloud. The thunder may be simply a change of weather or it could be the sound of a jet flying overhead to some other destination. The general direction of the poem is from the past to the present and then towards the future but this movement is not consistent, any more than the rhyme scheme is. Rhyme occurs throughout but without any predictable pattern; sometimes the rhymes gather together, sometimes they are quite widely spaced, as the thought comes and goes. The poet draws a contrast between the lack of direction in his own recent life and the compulsive, migratory habits of the wild geese. He has been 'up-and-down' and stuck in a 'grievous artifice' whereas they are described as 'Fanatic', 'Instinctive', and are seen in images of incisiveness: scissors and darts. Although the imitation French hotel has a vulgar commercialism which he dislikes, he is still reminded by it of holidays in France with his wife and the memory makes him aware of time and change. A time has come for decisions and he has learned from the example of the geese (lines 7–10), but his resolution to return to his old home (in Hull) seems qualified by the word 'trickles' (line 23) and the uncertainty of the final sentence. As the last line of the whole sequence in memory of his wife, it must seem to the reader to be addressed to her. However, the italics and the direct address, when he referred to her as 'She' earlier, alert us to understand that the poet is talking to someone else now, someone new with whom he has fallen in love. The shock to the reader of this revelation is considerable. It may be possible to hear the line as addressed both to his wife-to-be and to his dead wife, whose approval he seeks.

NOTES AND GLOSSARY:

Fife:	a region south of Dundee
up-and-down:	between Dundee and his house in Hull; perhaps also better and worse parts of experience, as in 'ups and downs'
flightpaths:	migrating geese follow the same routes north and south through Scotland each spring and autumn
Tay:	the river that flows through Dundee
make . . . way!:	an imitation of the call of the geese
Communal . . . scissors:	geese fly in large V-shaped formations
grievous artifice:	painful and contrived arrangement (with the suggestion of grief and perhaps also deception in an attempt to hide his grief)
two bridges:	the rail bridge and road bridge across the Tay
château . . . gables:	an imitation of French castles on the Loire, with elaborate pointed towers and ornamented roofs
expense account:	where the bill is usually paid by a company and not by the individual; the suggestion here is of pretentiousness and expense
baronial:	trying to look aristocratic; the word can be used of a Scottish style of architecture of an earlier period, also imitative of French castles
library:	store (of memories)
desk of rhymes:	desk at which he writes his poetry

Poems from *Northlight* (1988)

Elegies is a collection deriving from a special set of circumstances and, for that reason, is not an ordinary part of the development of Dunn's poetic career. With *Northlight* he resumes where *St Kilda's Parliament* left off. Many of the poems explore further his growing awareness of Scotland's past and, living as he does in an area rich in archaeological remains, he digs back into the Pictish and prehistorical layers. At the same time he locates more of his poems outside Britain, whether in Italy, Australia or the Congo, and uses these foreign perspectives to widen his own horizons and to comment on matters nearer home. Many of the poems are longer than those in the early collections: some are extended flights of fancy such as 'An Address to Adolphe Sax [the inventor of the saxophone] in Heaven'; some are meditations on weighty subjects, such as 'Memory and Imagination'. In a number of poems he writes surreal parables which may be compared to the parables in Seamus Heaney's *The Haw Lantern* (1987). Balancing these rather sinister forays are poems in which he celebrates love, the pleasures of his second marriage and a freer enjoyment of the landscape and area where he has settled down. He remains a poet of regular forms and writes in rhyme more than he did but he seems more at his ease and more accepting than he appeared to be in the early collections.

'Going to Aberlemno'

Some places, because of their architecture or because of events which happened there, remain fixed in the period of their construction or the events with which they are linked. To visit them is a journey in time rather than space.

COMMENTARY:
From the beginning there is a dislocation of the reader's ordinary expectations. 'Archaeologies' are usually sited in the ground but here they are 'of air'; 'Folkways' might be looked for in songs or folklore but here they are found in churches and physical areas. This confusing or reversing of the physical and the intangible continues throughout the three sentences and intricate rhyming of the poem. The ancient, mysterious world of the Picts can be approached by visiting a place with physical remains, but the visitor has to attend to elements beyond the seen and heard. Despite numerous traces of their carvings and constructions, remarkably little is known about the habits, beliefs and language of the old inhabitants of Scotland. From about the fifth century AD they began to lose their separate identity and their language, although in places, mainly in the eastern half of the country, they continued to erect carved stones displaying something of their culture. Aberlemno is one such place. Dunn travels back past the modern place to 'the previous/Country'. He uses a kind of cultural code,

apart from the dislocation mentioned above, to indicate that he is moving into a strange time. The four roads crossing in line 11 are strongly reminiscent of one of the best-known lines from classical Greek literature. In Sophocles's *Oedipus Rex* (fifth century BC) the murder by Oedipus of his father takes place where three roads meet: this detail is a crucial clue to the dilemma in the drama. The similarity of the two lines is striking: as in Sophocles we recognise that we have found something of importance. The next line of the poem refers to 'the tallest oak'. Again, although this detail is found in the twentieth century, the oak triggers a response to something beyond our century. The oak tree was sacred to the Druids, the priest class of the ancient Celtic world. Dunn is alerting the reader to a break-through into that earlier dimension, the 'essential east' where civilisation had its dawn. The kingdom and the Picts come alive through 'astral solitude', and the kings ride again on the sculptured stone. Many of the standing stones are aligned in relation to the moon, sun or stars and, although we are not sure what significance these alignments had for the Picts, the culture still leaves its special thumb-print, its cosmic signature in the landscape.

NOTES AND GLOSSARY:

Aberlemno:	a village in the east of Scotland
folkways:	traditions, customs of the people
kirks:	(*Scots*) churches
haar:	sea mist
essential:	unique
ill-starred/Inlets:	the ugly traces of developments which have failed
breaker's-yard:	a place where old machinery and cars are crushed for scrap
sore:	an ugly wound on the land
Above . . . Firth:	north of the Firth (estuary) of Tay

'Winkie'

The poem celebrates the achievement of Winkie, a homing-pigeon, which was used by a bomber crew in the Second World War to summon help when their plane was shot down off the coast of Norway. Dunn looks back in history and praises the exploits of pigeons in the service of human beings. Winkie, stuffed, is displayed in a glass case in the local museum in Dundee.

COMMENTARY:

The final line releases the pigeon which has been held in the poem. However, the whole poem is a flight of imagination, prompted by seeing the stuffed Winkie in the museum, and the irregular form with its indented lines is suggestive, in a mild way, of different wing movements. Rhyme does not feature but there are many repetitions of syntax, particularly in the final long paragraph, listings of attributes, and an unusually high proportion of the lines ending with an 's' sound. The compilation has an unforced, free-ranging quality in line with the way in which Dunn sees pigeons as unassertive, helpful and undevious. They ignore the divisions and regulations so binding on human beings, crossing frontiers and walls with impunity. It is precisely their instinctiveness and ordinariness that so appeal to Dunn and that he sees as the basis for their special symbolic status as described at the end of the poem. For pigeons, Carnoustie is as significant as Babylon, the urban allotment as attractive as the Chaucerian casement. In elevating pigeons, the poet exposes the pretensions and wasted energies of human beings, and it is because humans are so fanatical, scheming and cruel that he repeats his call: 'GIVE ME GOOD PIGEONS!' The poem is touching, amusing, chastening and inventively satisfying. The individual story is spliced into the more general presentation of pigeons.

NOTES AND GLOSSARY:

'We also serve':	motto on the Mitchell Medal, awarded to animals for bravery (equivalent to the Victoria Cross). In the sonnet 'When I consider how my light is spent', by John Milton (1608–74), the final line reads, 'They also serve who only stand and wait'
taxidermed:	stuffed, the external part of a dead animal processed to retain a life-like appearance
Municipal:	related to a small town; official (in the town's museum)
snapped:	photographed
mascot:	lucky charm
survival kit:	essential items for keeping alive in adverse circumstances
wooden bars:	of the cage for the pigeon in the bomber
fuselage:	main body of the aeroplane
your only nature:	the pigeon does not choose its action; instinct tells it to return home
dignitaries:	officially important persons in the city or the country district
bucolic:	of the countryside
Fife ... Mearns:	areas in the east of Scotland (near where the pigeon comes from)
microfilm:	film on which material can be recorded in miniature
Clandestinely:	in secret
Warsaw:	the capital city of Poland, scene of a bitter siege in the Second World War

Prussian:	a citizen of the former north German kingdom. In 1870–1 during the Franco-Prussian War Prussians laid siege to Paris, and pigeons were commonly used to carry messages in and out of the city
unvisa'd:	not possessing or requiring a visa, allowing a foreigner to enter
legionary:	soldier
dogsbodies:	persons doing general unskilled tasks
Dovecote:	a building specially designed for pigeons
spires:	towers and turrets in the ministry building
cushats . . . homers:	types of pigeon
cloak-and-dagger:	secret, engaged in spying
cryptography:	secret codes and their translation
Great Commoners:	great statesmen belonging to the House of Commons. 'The Great Commoner' was the nickname given to William Pitt the Elder (1708–78), English politician and orator
Nye Bevan:	Aneurin Bevan (1897–1960), a Welsh socialist prominent in British political life and noted for his powerful speeches
Gambetta:	Léon Gambetta (1838–82), a French Republican statesman prominent during the Franco-Prussian War (*see above*)
charts:	navigation charts
the Tay's dent:	the break in the Scottish coastline made by the estuary of the river Tay
Carnoustie:	a small town on the east coast of Scotland north of the Tay estuary from which the bird comes and to which it returns (homes) by instinct
ringed:	marked with details of the owner
tidings:	information, news
billet-doux:	a love letter (originally French)
jammed:	with the radio signal mechanically blocked so that it cannot be heard
Babylon:	the ancient kingdom in the Middle East which was conquered by Persians on horseback in about 538BC
Chaucerian casements:	the kind of high windows in medieval romances from which ladies look longingly for their lovers. The English poet Geoffrey Chaucer (1340–1400) wrote several long poems inspired by courtly love
allotments:	small areas of land in towns rented for cultivation. Pigeons were commonly kept in sheds on allotments
long race:	racing pigeons can cover huge distances before returning to their base

Olympic: the dove is one of the symbols of the Olympic sports movement and world peace

love bird: the turtle-dove is a symbol of contented love

Dove of the Annunciation: the dove is the symbol of the Holy Spirit, and sometimes appears in paintings of the Virgin Mary as the first intimation of the coming of Jesus

strange beam: in paintings of the Annunciation, or announcement of the forthcoming birth of Jesus, a beam or ray of light connects the dove to the Virgin Mary

lily: a symbol of purity which is often associated with the Virgin Mary

Mendicant: begging

'The War in the Congo'

The poem is concerned with the odd connections and disconnections between things, in this case between war in Africa, a stamp in a boy's collection in a village in Ireland, and a chance meeting in a bar in Glasgow.

COMMENTARY:

The poem can be divided into two equal halves which comment on each other. The first four stanzas consist mainly of the story told by the soldier; stanzas 5–8 consist of Dunn's thoughts on the boy who received the stamp and on the anonymous owner of the arm with the letter. Why the Irish ex-soldier tells the story is not made clear. Was he simply struck by the oddity of a dead arm holding a letter? It appears that he was not particularly curious: he did not specify whether the arm was male or female and, with a strange sense of morality or decency, he chose not to read the letter but saw nothing wrong with removing the stamp for his nephew. As Dunn tells us in the sixth stanza, his own concern is not centred on Africa but on the incongruity of the boy in Howth handling the stamp, unaware of the circumstances in which it was found. The shift to the present tense in this stanza indicates that the query in the poet's mind continues. The boy in all his stamp-collecting eagerness is connected with the situation in the Congo by the repeated phrase 'hot, hot and equatorial', but the connection exists in the poet's imagination, not in the boy's consciousness. 'That innocent know-nothing stamp, lonesome in history' has no intrinsic significance but it represents the interconnectedness of everything when one catches the random link, and the disconnectedness of things when the link is missing or unnoticed. The poem does not melodramatise the point; it accepts that the background history of the letter cannot be known. In its unemphatic steps, long line by long line, a link is made, a query is raised.

NOTES AND GLOSSARY:

Title: what had been the Belgian Congo in Africa became independent in 1960, and a brutal civil war followed which lasted till 1963. The territory is now divided between Zaïre and Congo-Brazzaville

Irish Army: as part of the United Nations force trying to establish peace in Congo, the Irish Army played a leading role

equatorial: on the equator, hot and humid

breeze-blocks: light building bricks made of cement and coke debris

Howth: a picturesque residential village on the Irish coast immediately north of Dublin

cleft stick: written messages in Africa were often carried by runners in the split end of a stick

Anon: the short form of anonymous, unknown person

with tweezers ... paper: the careful handling of the stamp, using the steam to unstick the glue and then drying the detached stamp

Philately: collecting postage stamps as a hobby

there: to a foreign country

Part 3

Commentary

Themes, style and development

In an interview (*Scotland on Sunday*, 11 March 1990), Dunn spoke of how the experience of writing *Elegies* gave him 'a greater sense of poetry as something almost sacred. Something that people share'. And he went on to say: 'I've always believed in writing – not for "the public", I've no idea who they are – but for other people. When you write only for yourself, all sorts of obscurity and self-indulgence creep in . . . the great curse of the modern arts.' It may seem curious that he should have become particularly aware of poetry as shared when he was writing his most personal poems. If we look back across his poetic career, the paradox may be resolved.

His first book, *Terry Street*, is oddly impersonal, as if he set himself like an apparatus to register and record the happenings around him. Of course, in the choice of happenings and the manner of the recording he does reveal himself as a specific sensibility but he does not draw attention to his self. Gradually, in his subsequent books, he becomes less reticent and writes more openly about his self-awareness, even when he feels very detached from other people, as in 'The Hunched'. In exploring his background, both familial and cultural, he reaches the springs of his emotional life. This discussion of his development can be presented as a question: could Dunn have written *Elegies* earlier in his career? The probability is that he could not have done. Without the large range of subjects, the determination to trace back attitudes, and a confidence in locating himself in relation to these attitudes – all manifested in *St Kilda's Parliament* – he could not have coped with the challenge of the tragic situation detailed in *Elegies*.

Dunn's poetry demonstrates a fascination with the values according to which people, including himself, live their lives and with the values which divide or unite societies. The poems set in Terry Street were prompted, in part, by the oddity in his eyes of the codes of behaviour around him. Ten years later he continued to be aware of being different and could write, 'In the community of accents and attitudes Hull represents, I still feel as if I'm not at home'.* Although he came from a working class background, the differences between his community in Inchinnan and Hull were more striking than any similarities. The emphasis in the poems is on squalor, grime and stunted lives: 'dog-shit under frost'; women who are 'often fat

*Quoted in *Nine Contemporary Poets: a Critical Introduction*, p. 221

and unlovely'; an atmosphere where 'layers of smell flake off the air like invisible soot'. It is not that Dunn is heavily judgmental in social or moral terms but neither is he sympathetic. Furthermore, Terry Street is curiously isolated in time and place as it appears in the poems, and he makes little attempt to diagnose its condition or investigate any explanatory background.

To his own Scottish background he is much more sympathetic. In 1979 he claimed: 'Over the years my writing has tried to keep a promise with a Scottish, rural working class background. It is a promise I don't remember making. What the precise nature of the promise is, I also don't know . . . To persevere with the art of poetry is to pick up a bet you made with yourself. Nationality and background are involved in the bet I made.'† Between 1969 and 1981, when he returned to live in Scotland, there was a gradual but definite increase in the number of poems examining different backgrounds. In the Terry Street phase he had learned to observe and describe surfaces, activities and patterns; when he came to look at himself more closely he felt an obligation to explain and this led to a fascination with the forces and circumstances which have shaped him. History books often used to be written as if only the rulers – who were almost always drawn from an aristocratic class – were of significance and had personalities requiring study. Douglas Dunn's poetry shares in a revolt against such a notion and tries to include less prominent people in the story of social evolution. In 'Portrait Photograph, 1915' he speaks as a common soldier:

> We too have our place, who were not photographed
> So much and then only in multitudes

The poet has gradually come to value locality more highly and he celebrates and commemorates the powers which give it an identity. In 'The Musician' he laments the loss to the community of carpentry and musical skills with the death of the fiddler, MacAuley. Locality is one of the main subjects in *St Kilda's Parliament* and *Northlight*.

Not that his concern with community is limited to a nationalist or personally parochial interest. Politically, his perspective is global. His long sequence poem *Europa's Lover* pulls together many centuries and all the continents in its anatomy of colonialism. Commerce, culture, war, exploitation, 'Accomplishments and guilts' jostle together in the sections of the poem. Who are the real barbarians – the conquered or the conquerors? Dunn's sympathies are not for the glories of empire but for the subjugated and the evicted. He sees that in a situation of exploitation, where one group rules and many work, most become accomplices in the iniquities and inequalities. A subservience is bred which accepts the

†Quoted in *Nine Contemporary Poets: a Critical Introduction*, p. 221

prevailing order as natural and inevitable and this is the deepest slavery. In 'Empires' the sour side of the poet pronounces:

> All men were fooled.
> It still persists. It will be so, always.
> Listen. An out-of-work apprentice plays
> *God Save the Queen* on an Edwardian flute.
> He is, but does not know it, destitute.

This poem from *Barbarians* is typical of many in the collection. Some people, of course, in any age try to ignore or defy the prevailing authority and Dunn sees writers like himself as subversives in the 'culture of connivance'.

He is aware that people who are suppressed and treated with contempt do not necessarily respond with patient rationality but often burst out in vindictive aggression. Some of the poems speak for this bitterness and, for example in 'The Sportsmen', relish a revenge against the oppressors:

> They will be murdered in bedrooms,
> Their cars pressed into squares of scrap.

The substantial poem 'The Happier Life' (not included in *Selected Poems*) offers an examination of his ambivalent idealism. In it he swings about from one untenable attitude to another. Sometimes he favours non-involvement: 'Wise apathy's a proper stance, aspiring/To wry complacencies of the retiring'; sometimes, a harsher cynicism breaks out:

> Community's a myth. We'll never find
> The man whose happier lives and peace of mind
> Outstay all changes

He has always been interested in imagining how other people think and feel, and his construction of dramatic personae in poems allows him the freedom to voice partial moods of his own and attitudes of others to which he would certainly not give his extra-poetic, wholehearted support. For this reason it is difficult, particularly in his earlier poetry, to establish categorically Dunn's socio-political position. As his career has developed, however, his standpoint has emerged more clearly, and he writes now from a more confident and worked-out socialist humanism. In the poem 'Poor People's Cafe's', accompanying his pamphlet (1990) against the Conservative government's community charge, he denounces the values implicit in 'Market Forces' and fears that the resulting situation where the richer become richer and the poorer become poorer leaves little scope for social responsibility: 'And it grows late for the decencies'. Religion and party-political orthodoxies play no part in his scheme of human betterment. In 'The Apple Tree' he explores various versions of salvation but in the end he concludes:

> Forge no false links of man
> To land or creed, the true are good enough. Our lives
> Crave codes of courtesy, ways of describing love,
> And these, in a good-natured land, are ways to weep,
> True comfort as you wipe your eyes and try to live.

Earlier, in the piece on himself quoted already, he had written: 'By temperament, I'm unwilling to be a "political poet". There are times, though, when everyone is led to go against the grain of what they expect of themselves. My imagination has tried to encompass political feeling – I don't like it, but imagination often does what the conscious mind may not particularly want it to do.'‡

When we look back at the major incidents and moves in Dunn's life, it is evident that he has profited poetically from them, even from the most negative ones. He has found ways of digesting very different experiences. One of the recurring motifs in his poetry is a weighing-up of losses and gains. If he was lonely or unhappy or out of place in Terry Street, he used his emotions for his work and succeeded in creating an authentic impression of such a place – a sort of heightened journalism. If he had decidedly mixed feelings about living in America and its capitalism, he could still explore these feelings more than a decade later in 'The Wealth', concluding:

> In your culture, I am a barbarian,
> But I'm that here, and everywhere,
> Lulled by alien rites, lullabyed with remorse
> Here on the backstreets of the universe.

Similarly, in relation to his native Scotland, he often senses a disinheritance: there seems to be more loss than gain in a land of 'disused workings', 'dead dominies [teachers]', 'discarded implements' and craftsmen made obsolete. Long before his first wife's death which led to *Elegies*, he had been often inclined to elegiac writing although, as he puts it in 'Maggie's Corner' (*Northlight*), he is usually acutely aware that, 'Nostalgia's a bam [daftness]. Distrust its stink.' One of his main impulses has been to rescue something valuable from dereliction. The act of memory is a recovery, and the poeticised memory or piece of research about the past is a resuscitation. The sequence of *Elegies* is, of course, the central example but there are many others such as 'Winter Graveyard', 'Unlucky Mariners', 'The Student', 'Elegy for the Lost Parish', 'St Kilda's Parliament', 'The Harp of Renfrewshire', 'Tannahill', 'John Wilson in Greenock, 1786' and 'Abernethy' (*Northlight*). Indeed, the past is needed as a corrective to glib assumptions of the present. In 'Memory and Imagination' (*Northlight*), he makes a request:

‡Quoted in *Nine Contemporary Poets: a Critical Introduction*, p. 225

> Past, guide
> My eye, my hand,
> And make me new;
> Open your mausoleums and subdue
> Novelty's blandishments.

And in 'Winkie' (*Northlight*) he revivifies the stuffed pigeon so successfully that we accept the ending: 'FLY, WINKIE, FLY!'

His style has changed markedly in several ways across his career. At the
beginning, although *Terry Street* was warmly praised by reviewers and he
was commended for establishing a 'personal voice', there is sometimes an
apprentice quality to the poems and the bits do not always fit together
consistently. Dunn comments on his early writing:

> At the time, my ideas of poetic technique were vague and uninformed
> ... whatever decision I made about poetic technique arose less from
> what I read, and more from a confrontation of what I lived and saw and
> felt with an overrated sophistication I got from books. These were my
> inhibitions of the time – avoid the classical pantheon like the plague;
> write not about childhood; write not, certainly about daffodils; never
> speculate on infinity from insufficient evidence; maintain a moderate
> degree of clarity, at least; do not invent when reality is good enough and
> lying to hand for the making of images; show more than you tell; do not
> push subjectively too much into the foreground of the poem ... But I
> suppose that, like other poets of my generation, I found it easier to know
> what I should not do, and strenuously difficult to discover a *positive*
> programme of aesthetic values.**

In keeping with this negative programme, this anxiousness to avoid sound-
ing pretentious, there are virtually no poems which discuss art in his
first two collections. An exception of sorts is 'A Faber Melancholy' (not
included in *Selected Poems*) where he describes himself with a mixture
of self-regard and irony as 'Horace with a view/Of the gasworks' and
suggests that if poets 'find wisdom, it's that art and love/Survive behind
the times to keep us sane'.

In his third collection, *Love or Nothing*, there are several poems concerned with poetry. Sometimes he still mocks the solemnity of high-falutin
culture but he does also face his function as a poet. In 'Clydesiders' he
aspires to follow the model of well made, robust ships:

> My poems should be Clyde-built, crude and sure,
>
> . . .
> A poetry of nuts and bolts, born, bred,
> Embattled by the Clyde, tight and impure.

**Quoted in *Nine Contemporary Poets: a Critical Introduction*, p. 222

In fact, his poetry over the succeeding years becomes considerably more sophisticated and enlarged in its themes and styles. He experiments with voices, and the texture of his writing becomes much more varied. Something of this progression is charted in the description of each volume in Section 2. Paradoxically, as his poetic ambitions have grown, his awareness of the inadequacies of language have become more acute. His grief in *Elegies* finds some relief in the writing of verses but he accepts that there is also a futility in writing:

> I shiver in the memory
> And sculpt my foolish poetry
> From thwarted life and snapped increase.
>   Cancer's no metaphor.   ('Anniversaries')

Nevertheless, it is precisely his pushing against the limits of metaphor that demonstrates the profundity of his later poetry.

Part 4

Hints for study

How to read and discuss poems

The study of poetry requires a particular intensity and discipline. Obviously, poems can be read casually and with pleasure and you should read widely and without undue anxiety about deep understanding or knowledge of how poems are constructed. Serious discussion of poems, however, happens only when students have attended very closely to the interaction of a number of factors which operate to create an effect in the reader's mind.

Not all poems are designed to be read aloud, but readers will come to a better understanding of the structure of a poem, in sound and sense, if it is read aloud. Douglas Dunn prides himself, quite properly, on his craftsmanship, and it would be futile for readers to seek to ignore or neglect the craft in his poems. A coordination has to be made or found by the reader between the sense of the words in their syntax, the punctuation, the lineation, the pattern of stressed syllables, the recurring sounds and rhymes. Such a coordinated reading aloud is an appreciation and, at least, the basis of an understanding of the poem. The larger your own experience is of reading a wide variety of poems, the easier this act of coordination becomes.

Students often feel (or are made to feel) that the analysis of a poem requires an elaborate and very technical vocabulary. This is not so. A good analysis, however, does require to be precise: you need to be able to describe accurately what you perceive in the poem with your eyes and ears and to detail the interaction of the poem and your mind. You may, indeed, discover that the 'technical' terms, for example, of prosody, do have some advantages of economy, because they are accepted by poets and other critics as having a defined meaning. A good analysis also needs a balance between points or opinions and evidence from the poem in support of these points. See your answer in essay or examination as an argument, like a case made out by a lawyer: you summon witnesses from the poem to provide evidence for your contentions.

Some guidelines on approaching a new poem

(1) If the author and date of the poem to be studied are known (as is the case with Douglas Dunn's poems), it makes little sense not to find

out what you can about the author's life and situation. Remind yourself, however, that a poem is a contrivance and not a direct transcription of an incident in a biography or autobiography.

(2) Read the poem aloud a number of times, preferably over a period of some days, letting it work on you. You may find it helpful to read some other poems written by the poet at the same time.

(3) Jot down what you can tell about the poem as an arrangement of words on a page. Is the whole divided into equal or unequal sections or is it undivided? Are the lines all the same length or do they vary following some pattern? Is rhyme used? Is there a regular pattern of stressed syllables and do any sounds recur? Do the sentences vary in length and syntax and do they fit with the lines and the rhyme scheme? Notice the punctuation. This awareness of the physical layout is often a valuable way into the organisation of the thoughts and feelings in the poem.

(4) Look up any words and references which are unfamiliar to you.

(5) Identify the situation in which the poem is set and the nature of the speaker. Look out for any shifts in mood or tone of voice or speaker or kind of language or tenses of verbs. Pay particular attention to odd, unexpected combinations of words; they often mark pivotal points or points of complexity.

(6) Poems do not function simply in a line-by-line sequence. Images, sounds and tones echo and resound across the whole poem and the meaning is in this criss-cross mesh.

(7) What pressures is the poem exerting on your mind? Where in the poem are the sources of these pressures? What is the overall pressure or conflict of pressures coming from the poem?

Approaching essay and examination questions

(1) Read the question several times and write down what you see as problematic or contentious terms in the question. For example, if the question asks you to discuss 'irony' or 'realism' or 'sentimentality', you need to think about these terms and offer some working definition of them. Determine what the question is asking you to do. Is it a very specific question or a more general one? Do you need to agree with what it seems to imply? Think critically about what may be the assumptions in the question.

(2) Plan your answer. In your introduction you should discuss the question and lay down how you propose to proceed. The bulk of your essay should be built around a few main points (not too many) in response to the demands of the question. These points are based on your understanding and appreciation of the poems specified by the question. For each of the points you require appropriate quotations

and examples from the poetry; this is your evidence. The points should be in an order which suggests a developing line of argument leading to an inevitable conclusion, your answer to the question.

(3) Avoid unnecessary or irrelevant information and opinions. Be economical in your planning and your writing. Ration your use of abstract terms and avoid large claims about people or history or poetry. Do not separate the sound from the sense of the poetry; discuss how they work together.

(4) Think out your essay in paragraphs so that the examiner can see clearly when you move from one topic to another. Try to vary the syntax in your sentences.

(5) Read over what you have written and correct any mistakes tidily.

Sample questions

(1) Choose one of the Terry Street poems (*Selected Poems, 1964–1983*, pp. 3–19) and examine how the poet organises the details.

(2) Using two or three of the Terry Street poems (*Selected Poems 1964–1983*, pp. 3–19), discuss the attitudes of the observer. Do you consider the observer sympathetic or antipathetic to what is presented?

(3) Examine 'A Poem in Praise of the British' and explain why and how Dunn uses irony.

(4) Discuss Dunn's attempts to evoke childhood in 'After the War' and 'Boys With Coats'. Do you find his attempts convincing?

(5) Some notion of 'barbarians' keep appearing in Dunn's earlier poetry. Discuss this notion by considering the poems 'Guerrillas', 'Under the Stone', 'The Come-on' and 'In the Grounds'.

(6) Discuss the mixture of realistic and surrealistic elements in 'Ballad of the Two Left Hands' and comment on Dunn's use of a ballad metre.

(7) Explain the epigraph, a quotation from Luther, in 'The Apple Tree' and demonstrate its relevance to the overall meaning of the poem.

(8) In 'Green Breeks' Dunn presents a confrontation between the young Sir Walter Scott and Green Breeks. What is represented by the two figures and how does the poet present their struggle?

(9) When Dunn writes poems set in a period of the past, what is he trying to achieve? Base your answer on either 'Tannahill' or 'John Wilson in Greenock, 1786'.

(10) Attempt to describe the main strands of thinking in *Europa's Lover*. What does the poet appear to be arguing?

(11) Do you consider Dunn guilty of self-pity and sentimentality in *Elegies*? Use evidence from two or three poems in support of your view.

(12) Can you trace a progression in *Elegies*? Consider shifts in time,

action, mood and language through the sequence (as represented in *Selected Poems, 1964–1983*).

(13) The three poems in *Selected Poems, 1964–1983*, pp. 237–9, are sonnets. Discuss the interaction of form and content in the three poems. Why do you think Dunn is attracted to the sonnet form?

(14) Discuss the mixture of personal and impersonal, emotional and imaginative, straightforward and artificial in 'The Stories'. Does the poem achieve a balanced conclusion?

(15) How does humour feature in Douglas Dunn's poetry? You might consider, for example, lighter poems such as 'Ode to a Paperclip', satirical poems, and the use of humour as a counterbalance to solemnity.

(16) Can you discern consistent political attitudes in Dunn's poetry? Explore the consistency or the shifts of attitude across the poetry.

(17) Comment on the move from urban to rural imagery in Dunn's poetry. Does the move involve a change in values?

(18) Discuss the presentation of women in Dunn's poetry.

(19) Is 'class-consciousness' a useful term in discussing Dunn's poetry? Examine, with examples, its usefulness and any limitations you see.

Sample answer

Question

Do the poems in *Elegies* provide a consolation for the loss of a loved one? Concentrate your discussion on two of the poems.

Plan

INTRODUCTION: examine the question
can poems provide consolation? art as therapy?
discuss 'consolation'
consolation for the poet or for the reader?
choose poems but stress whole sequence

MAIN POINTS: expressing grief as release
recalling cherished moments as of continuing worth
possibility of reaching an understanding of loss
struggle with verse and language as positive

CONCLUSION: sense of some consolation for the poet
sense of consolation in reader
Dunn does move on at the end
but death is absolute

The simple wording does not conceal several major difficulties in the question. It is generally known that Douglas Dunn wrote the poems some time after the death of his wife from cancer at the age of thirty seven, and different poems derive from various aspects of his bereavement: they are not tidily consistent with one another. The question asks: 'Do the poems in *Elegies* provide a consolation?' but another question lurks behind it: Can the poems or any poems provide consolation for such a loss? Dunn has some doubts on the subject: 'I shiver in the memory/And sculpt my foolish poetry' ('Anniversaries'). And does the question refer to the poet's consolation or that of the reader? Art has often been discussed as a form of therapy – indeed, this is one of the oldest and most widely held theories of writing and reading – but it has proved very difficult to show how or if some therapy actually works in a particular case. Whatever consolation is available to human beings for the loss of a loved one, poetry (or art) can claim no monopoly but certain elements in certain poems may afford some particular comfort. I have chosen to look at 'Birch Room' and 'The Clear Day' while acknowledging that no two poems can stand for the whole sequence with all its changes in time, mood and focus.

One way in which many people find relief from grief is to relate the details of what happened to cause such pain. To express one's suffering can mean to relieve the pressure of the build-up of such feelings. This tendency is not very obvious in the two poems chosen for this essay but it does occur in some of the early poems of the sequence such as 'Second Opinion', 'Thirteen Steps and the Thirteenth of March' and 'Arrangements'. In the third of these there is even a grim, black humour when the poet enters the wrong part of the Registrar's office; he has come to register the death of his wife but finds himself, by mistake, at the desk for registering marriages. The cycle of registering births, marriages and deaths carries on in its bureaucratic way. The individual is tabulated but anonymous. Each experience is unique to the individual but also part of a shared process, and this duality is partly chilling, partly comforting: 'I feel myself digested in statistics of love'.

The second kind of consolation discovered in the poems stems from recalling cherished moments of a past when the loved one was happy. Such memories help to realign the present. 'Birch Room' is very much concerned with an attempt to balance the situation in which the poet finds himself now with a recollection of a pleasure he shared with his wife when she was alive. In fact, there are several related elements to be balanced in the poem: the outside and the inside of the house; the spring with its leaves and the bare winter; nature and art; we and I. The balancing is intimated in the title and reinforced by the tidy stanzas with their constraining, unforced rhymes. The centre of the balancing act in the past was his wife. Her 'modern inwit' (sensibility and understanding) combined with nature to 'Create a furnished dusk, a room like art'. It is this shared good place that Dunn tries to preserve by leaving the room unaltered and by writing the poem to celebrate the 'Birch Room'. In the second poem, 'The Clear

Day', the past times are not directly recalled but there is a strong feeling that the delights described in the first two thirds recall occasions of shared pleasure: 'Long afternoons/Have been reduced [distilled] to this significant/Table'.

A curious feature of *Elegies* for many readers is that much of the poetry is neither macabre nor maudlin nor gloomy but pleasant and even enjoyable and very satisfying. Moreover, the enjoyment is not all set in a remembered, shared past but, in some poems, asserts itself in the present. There are two aspects to this. Gradually Douglas Dunn is able again to take pleasure in things around him, and also he finds that the pressure of these things counteracts his grief and pushes him towards a more balanced view of his whole situation. Both these aspects are apparent in 'Birch Room', where the birds in the 'Bud-studded' branches recall some piece of art by his wife and the first hint of the new leaves persuades him towards hope, 'an uncoerced/Surrender to the story of the Spring'. Winter does pass and, perhaps, a new life is possible for him. A sense of sharing is still very strong.

The opening of 'The Clear Day' is positive: 'Sunlight gathers in the leaves, dripping/Invisible syrups.' Most of the poem describes pleasurable experiences redolent of a tranquil summer afternoon in a familiar place. In the early lines words such as 'melodious', 'lazily' and 'languid' emphasise the gentle comfort, and in lines 11–20 the poet seems to transcend his physical location and enter an idyllic dimension. In lines 21–33 he is aware of his surroundings but simultaneously detached from them. Only in the final nine lines does something of his larger situation and his loss emerge when he imagines himself writing the poem (which we are reading) in 'the muddle of lost tenses'. And only in the fourth line from the end does he refer to his dead wife: 'I shall sieve through our twenty years' (of marriage). It is necessary to point out the proportions of the poem because, in the end, despite all the delightful sensations in the bulk of the composition, 'the sob in the intellect,/The truth that waits for me with its loud grief' is 'beyond understanding'. The pleasures, therefore, are perhaps not a sufficient consolation for the abiding sense of loss in Dunn. The phrase 'benign remorse' (line 20) anticipates something of his dilemma. For the reader, but not for the poet, the evocation of the pleasures of the clear day in summer outweighs the bleak emptiness of the night.

In the fifth line from the end of 'The Clear Day', the phrase 'radiantly painful speculations' carries the ambivalence of the poet's feelings: 'radiantly' can look back to the glories of the day while 'painful' goes with 'loud grief'. Poems seldom offer categorical answers to problems; if poets knew such answers, they might not feel compelled to write the poem. Part of a reader's pleasure in poetry is derived from sharing in the poet's feat of juggling. In *Elegies* Dunn challenges himself to find verbal formulae – images, cadences, verse forms for his confused state of mind. Over and over again he manages to engage our imaginative attention. Sometimes he succeeds because of the exactness of his observation and description, as in the surprising adjectives applied to the tits in 'Birch Room', 'Rotund and acrobatic', or in the wonderful evocation of simple sensations, mainly auditory, in lines 22–9 of 'The Clear Day'. The latter poem has a more complicated syntax than the former and a much greater variety of lengths of sentence but in both cases the pacing of the poetry seems beautifully judged. The pleasure a reader takes in the craft of the poetry is obviously a consolatory factor even when, as in 'The Clear Day', the concluding logic of the poem is gloomy.

In conclusion, it can be argued that some kinds of consolation for loss are provided by *Elegies*. Of course, the death of a loved one is, in an obvious sense, absolute and for that absoluteness there can be no cancelling consolation. However, in the sequence Dunn does change and his grief does come to be accommodated in a continuing sequence of events and emotions. It would be impudent to say how consoled he is by his own poems but a pattern does emerge and in the end he seems to be released into a new and different phase of his life. What we as readers judge is the effect not on the poet but on ourselves. We become involved in a sad situation by proxy or we read the poems as scenes in a drama. We wish to make sense of one of the most painful human situations. The positive elements in this drama do, overall, predominate, and it is fair to pronounce that the poems do provide consolation.

Part 5

Suggestions for further reading

Douglas Dunn's Poetry

Terry Street, Faber and Faber, London, 1969.
The Happier Life, Faber and Faber, London, 1972.
Love or Nothing, Faber and Faber, London, 1974.
Barbarians, Faber and Faber, London, 1979.
St Kilda's Parliament, Faber and Faber, London, 1981.
Elegies, Faber and Faber, London, 1985.
Selected Poems 1964–1983, Faber and Faber, London, 1986.
Northlight, Faber and Faber, London, 1988.
Poems, New and Selected, The Ecco Press, New York, 1989.
Dante's Drum-Kit, Faber and Faber, London, 1993.

Other works by Dunn

A Choice of Byron's Verse (ed. by Douglas Dunn), Faber and Faber, London, 1974.
Two Decades of Irish Writing (ed. by Douglas Dunn), Carcanet, Cheadle Hulme, 1975
Secret Villages, Faber and Faber, London, 1985.
Andromache, translated from Racine, Faber and Faber, London, 1990.
Poll Tax: The Fiscal Fake, Chatto and Windus, London, 1990.
Scotland: An Anthology (ed. by Douglas Dunn), Harper Collins, London, 1991.
The Faber Book of Twentieth-Century Scottish Poetry (ed. by Douglas Dunn), Faber and Faber, London, 1992.

Critical Studies (including interviews)

CRAWFORD, ROBERT and KINLOCH, DAVID (EDS): *Reading Douglas Dunn*, Edinburgh University Press, Edinburgh, 1992. A sound biographical chapter, eleven essays on the work, and a very thorough bibliography.
'Douglas Dunn Talking with Robert Crawford', *Verse*, no. 4, 1985.
HAFFENDEN, J.: *Viewpoints: Poets in Conversation with John Haffenden*, Faber and Faber, London, 1981.

HULSE, M.: 'Order, benevolence, love', *Prospice*, 17, 1985.

KING, P. R.: *Nine Contemporary Poets: a Critical Introduction*, Methuen, London, 1979.

SAIL, L: 'The Politics of Grief', *Prospice*, 19, 1986.

WILLIAMS, D.: ' "They will not leave me, the lives of other people": the Poetry of Douglas Dunn', *Studies in Scottish Literature*, 23, 1989.

The author of these notes

ALASDAIR D. F. MACRAE was educated at the University of Edinburgh and taught for a short time in secondary schools before taking up a lectureship in the University of Khartoum, Republic of Sudan. He is now Senior Lecturer in English Studies at the University of Stirling. He has edited *Selected Poetry and Prose of Shelley* (Routledge) and is about to publish *Yeats: A Literary Life* (Macmillan). He has written widely on modern poetry. He is the author of the York Notes on *Macbeth*, *The Waste Land* and *Selected Poems of Shelley*.

Index

The index gives an alphabetical listing of the poems discussed in Part 2.

York Notes: list of titles

CHINUA ACHEBE
Things Fall Apart

EDWARD ALBEE
Who's Afraid of Virginia Woolf?

MARGARET ATWOOD
The Handmaid's Tale

W. H. AUDEN
Selected Poems

JANE AUSTEN
Emma
Mansfield Park
Northanger Abbey
Persuasion
Pride and Prejudice
Sense and Sensibility

SAMUEL BECKETT
Waiting for Godot

ARNOLD BENNETT
The Card

JOHN BETJEMAN
Selected Poems

WILLIAM BLAKE
Songs of Innocence, Songs of Experience

ROBERT BOLT
A Man For All Seasons

CHARLOTTE BRONTË
Jane Eyre

EMILY BRONTË
Wuthering Heights

BYRON
Selected Poems

GEOFFREY CHAUCER
The Clerk's Tale
The Franklin's Tale
The Knight's Tale
The Merchant's Tale
The Miller's Tale
The Nun's Priest's Tale
The Pardoner's Tale
Prologue to the Canterbury Tales
The Wife of Bath's Tale

SAMUEL TAYLOR COLERIDGE
Selected Poems

JOSEPH CONRAD
Heart of Darkness

DANIEL DEFOE
Moll Flanders
Robinson Crusoe

SHELAGH DELANEY
A Taste of Honey

CHARLES DICKENS
Bleak House
David Copperfield
Great Expectations
Hard Times
Oliver Twist

EMILY DICKINSON
Selected Poems

JOHN DONNE
Selected Poems

DOUGLAS DUNN
Selected Poems

GERALD DURRELL
My Family and Other Animals

GEORGE ELIOT
Middlemarch
The Mill on the Floss
Silas Marner

T. S. ELIOT
Four Quartets
Murder in the Cathedral
Selected Poems
The Waste Land

WILLIAM FAULKNER
The Sound and the Fury

HENRY FIELDING
Joseph Andrews
Tom Jones

F. SCOTT FITZGERALD
The Great Gatsby
Tender is the Night

GUSTAVE FLAUBERT
Madame Bovary

E. M. FORSTER
Howards End
A Passage to India

JOHN FOWLES
The French Lieutenant's Woman

ELIZABETH GASKELL
North and South

WILLIAM GOLDING
Lord of the Flies

GRAHAM GREENE
Brighton Rock
The Heart of the Matter
The Power and the Glory

THOMAS HARDY
Far from the Madding Crowd
Jude the Obscure
The Mayor of Casterbridge
The Return of the Native
Selected Poems
Tess of the D'Urbervilles

L. P. HARTLEY
The Go-Between

NATHANIEL HAWTHORNE
The Scarlet Letter

SEAMUS HEANEY
Selected Poems

ERNEST HEMINGWAY
A Farewell to Arms
The Old Man and the Sea

SUSAN HILL
I'm the King of the Castle

HOMER
The Iliad
The Odyssey

GERARD MANLEY HOPKINS
Selected Poems

TED HUGHES
Selected Poems

ALDOUS HUXLEY
Brave New World

HENRY JAMES
The Portrait of a Lady

BEN JONSON
The Alchemist
Volpone

JAMES JOYCE
Dubliners
A Portrait of the Artist as a Young Man

JOHN KEATS
Selected Poems

PHILIP LARKIN
Selected Poems

D. H. LAWRENCE
The Rainbow
Selected Short Stories
Sons and Lovers
Women in Love

HARPER LEE
To Kill a Mockingbird

LAURIE LEE
Cider with Rosie

CHRISTOPHER MARLOWE
Doctor Faustus

ARTHUR MILLER
The Crucible
Death of a Salesman
A View from the Bridge

JOHN MILTON
Paradise Lost I & II
Paradise Lost IV & IX

SEAN O'CASEY
Juno and the Paycock

GEORGE ORWELL
Animal Farm
Nineteen Eighty-four

JOHN OSBORNE
Look Back in Anger

WILFRED OWEN
Selected Poems

HAROLD PINTER
The Caretaker

SYLVIA PLATH
Selected Works

ALEXANDER POPE
Selected Poems

J. B. PRIESTLEY
An Inspector Calls

WILLIAM SHAKESPEARE
Antony and Cleopatra
As You Like It
Coriolanus
Hamlet
Henry IV Part I
Henry IV Part II
Henry V
Julius Caesar
King Lear
Macbeth
Measure for Measure
The Merchant of Venice
A Midsummer Night's Dream
Much Ado About Nothing
Othello
Richard II
Richard III
Romeo and Juliet
Sonnets
The Taming of the Shrew
The Tempest

Troilus and Cressida
Twelfth Night
The Winter's Tale

GEORGE BERNARD SHAW
Arms and the Man
Pygmalion
Saint Joan

MARY SHELLEY
Frankenstein

PERCY BYSSHE SHELLEY
Selected Poems

RICHARD BRINSLEY SHERIDAN
The Rivals

R. C. SHERRIFF
Journey's End

JOHN STEINBECK
The Grapes of Wrath
Of Mice and Men
The Pearl

TOM STOPPARD
Rosencrantz and Guildenstern are Dead

JONATHAN SWIFT
Gulliver's Travels

JOHN MILLINGTON SYNGE
The Playboy of the Western World

W. M. THACKERAY
Vanity Fair

MARK TWAIN
Huckleberry Finn

VIRGIL
The Aeneid

DEREK WALCOTT
Selected Poems

ALICE WALKER
The Color Purple

JOHN WEBSTER
The Duchess of Malfi

OSCAR WILDE
The Importance of Being Earnest

THORNTON WILDER
Our Town

TENNESSEE WILLIAMS
The Glass Menagerie

VIRGINIA WOOLF
Mrs Dalloway
To the Lighthouse

WILLIAM WORDSWORTH
Selected Poems

W. B. YEATS
Selected Poems